Conversations with Frank Waters

Conversations with Frank Waters

edited by
John R. Milton

SAGE BOOKS

THE **SWALLOW PRESS** INC.
CHICAGO

First Edition
First Printing

Published by
The Swallow Press Incorporated
1139 South Wabash Avenue
Chicago, Illinois 60605

ISBN (CLOTH) 0-8040-0575-3
ISBN (PAPER) 0-8040-0576-1
Library of Congress Catalog No. 78-189195

Chapter IV was originally published in *South Dakota Review,*
Spring 1971.
Grateful acknowledgement is made to Bob Kostka for permission to
use his photographs of Frank Waters. All rights reserved.

Contents

A Personal Note

When I first went to Taos, New Mexico about ten years ago, the most important thing I had in mind was finding and meeting Frank Waters. It was said that he lived quietly, without a telephone, outside a small Spanish village on the edge of the Pueblo land, and that he did not like to be bothered by people. He came into Taos occasionally for his mail or to buy groceries, but he was not to be confronted by a stranger from the North. In fact, it was impossible. So I was told.

I did not believe all that I heard. After letting word get out that I wished to meet the unapproachable Mr. Waters, I settled down to reading *The Man Who Killed the Deer* in a motel located just a mile from the pueblo where most of the book took place and only a few blocks from the old trading post which also figured in the novel. Two days later, after the unforgettable experience of reading a novel in its own setting, there was a knock at the door. It was Frank Waters, tall, lean, windburned, tan, looking very much like Robinson Jeffers, or an Indian. And friendly. His smile and his upward rolling eyes were impish; his voice was calm and settled like the land itself; and, also like the land, he was open and real.

There are few men with whom I feel as spiritually comfortable as I do with Frank Waters. Since that first meeting we have sat often in his adobe house at Arroyo Seco or out on the grass near the little stream that flows down the mountain, looking into space, thinking, talking without words. But the words are there, like the ever-present land of which Frank is so much a part. And they are useful words, valuable words, solid words, never flashy or artificially noisy like the words of too much contemporary literature.

A large part of Frank's appeal to me lies in his land-based and Indian-oriented mysticism. The premise for this mode of thought

1

and behavior is deceptively simple: living with the land. Not against it, or on it, or near it, but *with* it. This feeling runs throughout Waters' novels and most of his other writing, and it is precisely this feeling that has alienated readers who might be called Eastern, or metropolitan, or urban, or sophisticated. Curiously, the alienation between East and West in the realm of literature and of human behavior is very much like the alienation between Freud and Jung, the two foremost psychologists of our century. Eastern fiction is clearly Freudian, and Frank Waters is just as clearly Jungian. It is not surprising to find a Jungian analyst from Zurich visiting in Taos and usually in Frank's company. Jung himself visited the Taos Pueblo years ago and found it a fascinating place.

All of which is to suggest that Frank Waters, both man and writer, is highly attuned to the spiritual life of the Indian, to the religions based on the land and on the acceptance of nature. He is a believer, and we have been sadly short of believers for the past half-century.

It seemed necessary to me that Frank's opinions and attitudes be preserved, made available, outside his books. This would include, then, comments on his books, which would be of value to his readers as well as to scholars and critics who were examining his work. And so I asked the man who had been called unapproachable and who had become my close friend what he thought of sitting for three hours in front of television cameras, under hot lights, answering questions and chatting about himself and his work. With a few mild reservations, he agreed, and early in November, 1964, he showed up at the KUSD-TV studios in Vermillion, South Dakota, with a bad cold, a hoarse voice, and as much enthusiasm as he could muster under the circumstances.

We agreed to avoid all formal preparations. We wanted the talk to be as spontaneous as possible while covering all the important subject areas. Only once did I ask him a question which went unanswered, as I knew it would. I asked whether he had taken part in a kiva ceremony, knowing full well that a man who has indeed done so cannot talk about it. I simply wanted this on the record, if for no other reason than to indicate Waters' sincere ethical relationship with the Indians. Other than that, we talked at will, bothered only by Frank's cold, which became worse and turned to laryngitis so that we had to call the doctor between programs, and, later, by my own cold.

What was said during those three hours of conversation under the hot lights during several cold November days appears in the following text almost exactly as spoken.* Very little editing has been done except for a few factual matters which do not always get the proper attention in an informal conversation. A few more books have been published since 1964, but what appears in this text is the essential Frank Waters.

I wish only to express my deep gratitude to him, now, for helping to make this book, for being a good friend, and for the many insights which he has helped me to find. This book is, of course, really his.

John R. Milton
Vermillion, S.D.

---

*During the sixth conversation we were joined by Karen Kling, a USD graduate student; for the seventh conversation, we had with us Frederick Manfred, himself a distinguished novelist.

One

Milton: Your grandfather, who came from the southeastern part of the country, you said was somewhat the model for Joseph Rogier in the three novels which deal with the Pike's Peak area. Would you say that he, probably as much as anybody else in your family, is the one from whom you got your interest in the mountains as an area, or is this something that comes entirely out of your having lived by Pike's Peak for twenty to twenty-five years?

Waters: I think it is an individual thing. You don't get that from anyone. My father, for example, didn't like the mountains. He preferred to go out on the plains, at least in Colorado—go out there in a buckboard. He just loved to sit and watch the wind blow through the prairie grass. He was always uncomfortable in the mountains.

Milton: But not your grandfather?

Waters: My grandfather loved the mountains.

Milton: And this was what eventually pulled him into looking for gold?

Waters: Probably.

Milton: Did he ever feel resentful about someone like Stratton for striking it rich while he didn't?

Waters: No. This gold thing—you can't feel resentful because it is so crazy. A few blocks from our house there was a fellow called Jones who owned a drug store, a pharmacist by trade. When the

5

gold strikes were being made in Cripple Creek, he decided to go up one Sunday when the store was closed, and discover a gold mine. So he rode up on the little train, and wandered up in the hills. Seeing some prospectors and miners standing around, he said, "Well, boys, how do I find a gold mine?" They said, "Well, Mr. Jones, just stand up here on the ridge and throw your hat down into the gulch and wherever the hat lands, go down and dig." So this druggist threw his hat down, then promptly went down and staked out a claim where his hat had fallen. He struck a gold vein and the mine was named The Pharmacist, becoming one of the richest producing mines in the district of Cripple Creek. So the old saying was that "the mining men are all trying to find gold where it should be, and all the fools and tenderfeet are finding it where it is."

Milton: And this was the feeling that took hold of the whole community. Somewhere along the way, in the novels that you have written based somewhat on your grandfather, gold for him becomes something other than the money.

Waters: Yes, that's right.

Milton: You have him digging into the heart of Pike's Peak, where he can find out what makes Pike's Peak tick.

Waters: That grew into an obsession. The same sort of an obsession, I suppose, that Ahab had for Moby Dick. It's more than a white whale, it's more than gold.

Milton: Robinson Jeffers, later on, as you recall, as a poet had a good deal to say about the meaning within the rock, the rock holding the ancient traditions of the world and becoming almost human in this respect. Now is this something like Rogier was trying to find as he went into the Peak?

6

Waters: I think everyone is trying to find a meaning in life. They search for it in the medium that is most familiar to them.

Milton: He might have done the same thing somewhere else if he had settled somewhere else.

Waters: That's right.

Milton: But for yourself—because you have been in or around the mountains most of your life—has the mountain, Pike's Peak or Taos Mountain, the mountain as a kind of generic term, become specially significant to you? Could you get along without mountains now?

Waters: No. I am used to mountains. I love to have a mountain in my backyard. Right out the window all the time.

Milton: What about the Indians themselves—the Pueblo of Taos, let's say—do they have a special feeling for the mountains above them?

Waters: Well, I'll tell you. There is a wonderful old gentleman whom I know. His name is Dr. W. Y. Evans-Wentz. As an Oxford scholar he did a book on Celtic lore. Then he went to Egypt to study egyptology. Finally, he settled in Tibet, producing the world's four basic volumes on Tibetan Buddhism. When I last saw him, he was back in this country, very old, and compiling a book on the sacred mountains of the world. Explaining how certain mountains in all continents and countries always have been regarded as sacred, vast repositories of psychic energy. The influence of mountains on all peoples throughout the world is especially marked among the Indians in this country. Almost every Indian tribe I know in the Southwest reveres a certain mountain, as Pike's Peak. The Navaho homeland is bounded by the four sacred mountains, one each on the north, south, east and west. Even our people in Taos still conduct secret ceremonies in the mountains above the pueblo.

7

Milton: The same way.

Waters: It seems to be universal among all people.

Milton: Mountains more than water? The Blue Lake of the Taos Indians too, do they separate that from the mountains at all?

Waters: Water, like earth, is one of the four living elements embodied in all forms of life. Blue Lake takes on added significance because it lies just below the summit of the highest peak in the Sangre de Cristo mountains of New Mexico.

Milton: Simply part of the mountain.

Waters: Yes.

Milton: After you had left Colorado Springs and had had the experiences on the Mexican border with the particular Chinaman who appears in *The Yogi of Cockroach Court,* were you conscious yet of the specific relationship between Oriental thought and that of the Indians?

Waters: No, that came later when I became interested in the parallels between Indian ceremonialism and the various Oriental religious philosophies.

Milton: But these parallels have turned up.

Waters: There are distinct parallels.

Milton: Now part of this whole feeling about the mountains comes out in one passage that I would like to read from your first book. I'll read it to refresh your memory. And this I think has not only to do with the Indians but the digging into the earth, to get the pulse of the earth too, and I am wondering what you think about this after having written six novels around it.

Waters: I—I haven't looked at these books for 20 years, I suppose.

Milton: This is from *The Wild Earth's Nobility,* the very first one in which Rogier and Boné—is that the way you pronounce his name?—are out together. One is a man and one is a young boy, at this point confronting the Indians for the first time. And this drum beat that comes through the passage reminds me very much of Mary Austin, about the earth's rhythms. "He had been standing but a moment when he became aware of the beat of a drum. As he knew it had been sounding in his ears since he left the road. As it had been sounding, in the same time, unceasing all afternoon. Like the heart of the dry hills, the sandy mesa, suddenly beating with life. It was exactly like the beat of the earth. Not cloying with the will to blend like that of a white man's syncopation, nor changeful, quick with the live rhythm of a Negro's heel of palm upon a drum, but steadily intermittent, unvarying in tone, and insistent." Sounds to me very much like Mary Austin—the Theory of Two Beats—the blood comes in. "Horribly insistent to something in his bloodstream that could not flow gently or smoothly around the sound. It beat out flat and incessant, like the sun's blows on the arid earth, boldly outlined like the dark crags against the sky; quick and vigorous like the sudden drenching rains." And then later on in that passage Rogier becomes uneasy about this drum beat: "The timeless rhythm of the drum, reverberant in the darkness, grew in his blood. Like the little group of onlookers gathered about the dancers below him, he was experiencing more than the ragged spectacle before him. He was believing with his blood, more than the capacity of his mind could ever admit." Now this reminds me of Vardis Fisher's and to some extent Alan Swallow's insistence that Western literature will not come into its own until it becomes rational. And yet here we have coming out of the earth itself, the Western earth, the belief of the blood, rather than that of the mind.

Waters: I wouldn't use the term "blood" now. I would use "instinct" as opposed to "rationality."

Milton: But it still leaves us with the problem.

Waters: I believe myself that indigenous people on all continents are attuned to their own land instinctively or unconsciously. The Negro drum beat is so much different from the Indian drum beat. I have a friend who as a young girl lived in Africa where her father was a missionary. Later she lived among the Navahos as a missionary herself. I would often listen to her beat out the drum beat, the African rhythm, showing how entirely different it was from our own Indian rhythm. It is entirely different because it does reflect the vibratory quality of the land itself. Now I think we white people, we Anglo-European white people, are not yet wholly attuned, as these indigenous Indians are, to their mother earth.

Milton: Can we learn how to do this?

Waters: I think we are learning, if that is the word. In our few generations here we Americans are being changed. We are no longer wholly white Europeans. We are already taking on certain qualities of the land itself.

Milton: Do you think, then, that we will let rationalism replace this instinct? Probably not.

Waters: That's the trouble. I think our culture is over-rational at present. Materialistic and excessively rational. We are losing that deep strength of instinct of the unconscious by relying almost completely upon our shallow rationality.

Milton: Now, would you suggest, and it sounds like an impossibility to start with, that it would be a good thing for all Anglo-

Americans to be Indians for a while? Learn some of these nebulous values, shall we say?

Waters: The young people we call hippies are already doing it. I think it is doing them a lot of good. I saw a film made by a friend of mine who had taken a group of retarded children between the ages of five and twelve years old, and had started them out to dance. They were so bound within themselves, so self-conscious, that they couldn't get on their feet or do anything. The teacher was very wise. She would start beating a little bit on a drum, asking them to clap their hands. Then after they had clapped their hands for a while, she would say, "Now just imagine the movement, that beat taking place in you. Then get on your feet and make simple motions." Well, at the end of a month or so these retarded children were dancing spontaneously, instinctively, to what they felt in the music. That's something we all should learn.

Milton: Speaking of music again, in *The Wild Earth's Nobility*, Boné is a musical composer. He obviously feels some of these things in music, but, as indicated over and over again, the effect of music on man remains a mystery. Are we involved, then, in something that will always be mysterious, this instinctual response to nature, or can we bring the rational mind to bear on this and try to resolve it?

Waters: The response of a person to music, the rhythm of nature, the movements of the stars, the phases of the moon, is embodied in the great mystery, I think.

Milton: And you think this mystery should remain?

Waters: I don't believe we can ever rationalize it out of existence.

Milton: Is this one of the big differences now between the white man's ritual in religious areas and the Indian's ritual?

11

Waters: I think so. I've seen little Indian children of five and they step right out and dance to a drum beautifully. But few of our children can get right out and dance to modern compositions on the piano.

Milton: And the Indian is quite content with his mystery?

Waters: It's a part of him.

Milton: Whereas the white man is not content. Now, do these things—of course, again I am concerned with how some of these values can be carried over to the Anglo-American civilization—in your own experience, didn't these things come very gradually to you from being around the Indians?

Waters: I have been around Indians so much that it just seems natural to me.

Milton: The move that you made from California ultimately got you to Mora. This is a Spanish-speaking community, you said?

Waters: Yes.

Milton: Rather than Indian. Was it with the Pueblo in Taos that you made your first real contact?

Waters: Yes, that's right. Of course, I knew Indians when I was a small boy in Colorado Springs. They used to have an annual encampment there, just west of town. They would pitch their tepees and would live there all summer. Before they were put on the reservation and not allowed to come back, there were some Indians all the time. As a matter of fact, they would sit around on the street corners in town, selling deer hides and bear skins and things like that.

Milton: That's where this last passage came from?

Waters: Yes.

Milton: One of your own experiences as a youth. The question, of course, is whether the values some of us feel in the West can ever be transmitted to people who don't live here.

Waters: I think our own emotional reaction can be transcribed.

Milton: Would you, for example, expect your books to teach Easterners? I know what you would say, "A writer doesn't write to teach."

Waters: No, but I think the only value of art is to pass on an emotional experience to others. They may not learn from it, yet by arousing an emotional reaction I think you accomplish your job either by painting, music, or the written word.

Milton: Let's go back again to the order of the books for just a moment. I am curious about the way the experiences jell in your mind. The very early experiences from the Colorado Springs area did get into your first three novels. And it was later, in your sixth novel, that you went back to the California-Mexican border areas. Why didn't that one get written earlier?

Waters: It was. I didn't make the last revisions until after I got back from Washington during the war, but it had been written before the Colorado mining novels.

Milton: Any special problems that carried it over that long?

Waters: Yes, there was a great problem because the principal character is a youth in his twenties, and I wanted to show his background as a small boy. But I was too inept to know how to bridge the gap—whether I should leave the early part, or bring it in as antecedent, or how. Mechanical problem.

Milton: A good deal of this material was based on your stay on the border?

Waters: Yes, I love that area.

Milton: You like it? Not as much as the mountains?

Waters: No, no.

13

Milton: Going back to *The Wild Earth's Nobility* again. Part of the problem that comes out here is that of the land being forbidding as well as inviting. Now, man can dig deeply into the mountain, be drawn to it for his entire lifetime, and yet he can be shaken and repelled by the land at the same time.

Waters: This ambivalence can't be easily solved. It reflects the problem of duality inherent in all our natures, both man and mountain. We each have a dark side and a light side, so the mountains can seem very benign and they can also seem very malignant.

Milton: To everyone?

Waters: We are attracted to and repelled by mountains, as we are by persons. The journals of explorers and pioneers attest to this.

Milton: When some writers get around to writing out of their own past experience they frequently put into the book a sensitive artistic person such as Boné, and let him carry part of the significance. So the question arises: does it take a special sensitive response to the land to feel any of these things?

Waters: No, I think anyone can feel it. I once knew a telephone repair man who worked on that desolate stretch of desert between Imperial Valley and the Colorado River. He used to go out in a specially equipped truck that would travel over sand, and inspect the toll line across the sand dunes. I discovered that he would always climb up a pole and do his work facing the crinkled desert mountains. I asked him why. He said, "I just can't turn my back on those mountains. Something may happen." He was afraid of those mountains. Well, here is a very simple man, yet the emotional impact of those mountains seemed to him evil. He wanted to keep them in view all the time.

Milton: So—how long had he lived there, to get this feeling?

Waters: About three years.

Milton: So it doesn't take long then.

Waters: No.

Milton: Now, you didn't spend as much as three years in southern California or in Mora, New Mexico?

Waters: Oh, I lived more than a year in Imperial Valley and several years in Los Angeles and Riverside before I left California.

Milton: The reason I ask is that out of the Colorado Springs experience—which amounted to what, some twenty years? you were born there? and finished college there?—

Waters: I spent a good deal of my young life up in the mining camp of Cripple Creek, twenty miles away. Actually a mile straight up and twenty miles away.

Milton: —and out of this you got three rather big novels, *The Wild Earth's Nobility, Below Grass Roots,* and *The Dust Within The Rock,* coming to something like fifteen hundred pages. Then, out of the shorter stay on the Mexican border, a shorter novel.

Waters: Well, I think all young writers when they write their first books are using all the personal experiences they can chuck into them. Anybody can write an autobiography—autobiographical novel, let's call it. The test is when you exhaust that personal stuff and get to writing about other people.

Milton: You think that it would be worth suggesting to beginning writers that they concentrate on their biographical material?

Waters: I think probably the stuff they know best they should write about first.

Milton: Well, it seems they have to, yes. Do you think, looking back, that those first three big novels could be cut down?

Waters: Sure, if I were to do them now, they wouldn't be nearly as long.

Milton: But you wouldn't go back and touch these?

Waters: I don't know. Usually when I do a book, then I'm through. I go on to something else. But Alan Swallow for years has been urging me to condense these first three novels into one long one-volume narrative.* Perhaps he is right. Poetry is probably different. Like *Leaves of Grass,* which Walt Whitman wrote and rewrote. But a novel is different. You've got to stop sometime.

Milton: Do you find that out of the first three novels in your trilogy, however, certain ideas hang over and appear sporadically throughout your later novels?

Waters: Yes, I think so. Most men have one or two basic motifs that are carried over.

Milton: And it probably comes, again, somewhat from your grandfather's—

Waters: Probably.

Milton: The mountains?

Waters: Probably.

Milton: The Ute Indians you said came down to camp outside of Colorado Springs. How much influence did they have on the mysticism that seems to come out of your view of the mountains?

Waters: Well, when you get into mysticism you are getting into something very squeasy because so-called mysticism is anathema to most of us excessively rational Americans. But if you do know anything about Indians, you have to accept it as a natural part of Indian nature. They believe in the intangible as strongly as we believe in the tangible. I wish there was another name for it, but it's just a fact of existence you can't ignore.

*Pike's Peak, 1971.

Milton: Did you find this leading to what is a very apparent difference between your first three novels and the next three? The first three are full of tangibles—the white man's materialism, going after the gold, etc.—whereas the three later novels center somewhat on the Indians. While they are still very sensuous with natural images, they don't have all of these tangibles.

Waters: Well, there again, the first three novels are written from autobiographical material—the young writer handling a great mass of material, a lot of which doesn't belong in the book, for I think they are too loaded—whereas the last three were written about different groups of people. *The Man Who Killed the Deer* is about the Pueblo Indians, and *People of the Valley* is about Spanish-Americans, and *The Yogi of Cockroach Court* is a third racial group, the Coyotes, Mestizos, the mixed-breeds. Three different ethnic peoples in the Southwest.

Milton: You perhaps have the feeling that you could never go back to the kind of novel that you did first.

Two

Milton: After you left Colorado College in Colorado Springs where you had been studying general engineering, you went to the lower part of California on the Mexican border as an engineer of some kind. This was the telephone company job?

Waters: No, I first went to the famous Salt Creek oil fields in Wyoming and worked there four months as a day laborer. There I met an old man of about seventy, a marvelous old character who had been a cook and a surveyor in Teddy Roosevelt's party many years before. As close to a mountain man in those days as we had. He was very old and had taken his lifelong savings and bought a little Star Roadster and he was going down to San Diego to spend the rest of his days with a married daughter. But he couldn't drive the Star Roadster so he asked me to drive him to California. The trip sounded very entrancing to me. We had very little money, but he assured me I would not need an overcoat because it was sunny all the time, and whenever I was hungry I had only to reach up and pluck an orange or a banana. So we drove out to Los Angeles. Here he left me and went on his way. Finally I got a job with the telephone company and was sent down to the twin-town of Calexico-Mexicali on the Mexican border in Imperial Valley. This was a wonderful locale at that time.

Harry Chandler of the *Los Angeles Times* was developing vast expanses of desert south of the border in Lower California for cotton. It was irrigated by Colorado River drainage that then drained down below sea level into the American side of the border. At that time engineers were trying to talk up the All-American Canal which would bring the water straight into Imperial Valley.

19

But the *Los Angeles Times,* of course, was bucking the Boulder Dam, the All-American Canal, so that the Chandler interests could get all the water first. What was interesting to me at that time was not these political considerations, but the fact that the governor of Lower California, and Chandler, in order to get cheap labor, were bringing in shiploads of Chinese coolies and there were a number of wonderful stories of what happened.

A few years before, they had brought a whole shipload of Chinese coolies and Mexican peons from a little port on the west coast of Mexico called Topolobampo to work in the cotton fields just below Mexicali, and that was the first time I had heard about the famous tidal bores of the Colorado River. The steamer arrived at the mouth of the Colorado in the light of the full moon when the bores were very strong. The ship with about one hundred fifty of these coolies and peons was hit by these tidal bore waves and they were all drowned. But Mexicali was so interesting because that was the Chinatown par excellence.

Milton: This was perhaps the first big Chinatown on the West Coast, wasn't it?

Waters: Not the first, but the best. There was a very fine Chinatown in Los Angeles, and the one in San Francisco is very famous. That in Mexicali was practically unknown, but, to me, far more the real thing. Because thousands of these poor Chinese would come and wait there, doing almost anything to be slipped into this country.

Milton: All having been brought there directly by Chandler and the governor of Lower California, is that it?

Waters: And by powerful Chinese tongs in San Francisco.

Milton: And they picked them up in China.

Waters: Yes. They would bring a shipload at a time. And what they would do was to keep these Chinese there until they could be slipped a few at a time across the border, usually under the false bottom of a big produce truck. They would be taken up to Ferguson Alley in the old Chinatown of Los Angeles, which is where the modern railroad station is, and kept a few days until they revived. Then they would be sent up to San Francisco. This was all handled by the tongs. These Chinese laborers would have to spend the rest of their lives paying off their transportation. So there were thousands of Chinese in this Mexican town of Mexicali. It was full of bars, cantinas, opium places, and marijuana dens of all descriptions. It was a very unsafe place, but it was a very colorful place too.

Milton: This is where you got the material for *The Yogi of Cockroach Court*—the oddest title, perhaps, of any of your novels.

Waters: Cockroach Court got its name from the Mexican idiom which calls prostitutes *cucarachas* or "cockroaches." So the main red light district was known as the "Plaza de Cucarachas" or Cockroach Court. On the edge of this district lived the Yogi. His name was Tai-Ling, an old Chinese man, a very fabulous character. I suppose he was—you can't tell an Oriental's age by his looks, but he must have been about seventy. He had a little shop, a wonderful little shop where he sold herbs and such things. Ostensibly he made his living selling fish brought up the Colorado River from the Gulf of California. On the side he peddled opium and in the cellar he hid the—you might call them the wet-back Chinese. I got interested in the old man. I'd wander in there—his shop was like a movie set because he was interested in fish—you know Chinese love fish, interested in collecting odd types of fish and marine life. So all the boat masters and fishermen who would get a peculiar catch would bring it to him in a tin can or something, until his vast cluttered shop was full of tin cans, bottles, and aquariums of strange fish. Tai-Ling was quite a philosopher too, a Buddhist, and I thought he was quite a wonderful old man. The Yogi of Cockroach Court.

Milton: Does he exist in the novel pretty close to the original person? That is, have you transcribed him quite accurately?

Waters: He is taken almost wholly from life and, as a matter of fact, I didn't know how to end the book—it was published several years after I wrote it. I had some trouble with it. But the ending was written for me about two years after I left there, before the book was published, when I saw a clipping from the local newspaper. The Mexican rurales or rural police and American immigration officers had instituted a raid on his place, completely surrounding it, and blowing up the shop with a bomb when he refused to come out. The ending was written for me, actually.

Milton: The ending except for the epilogue.

Waters: Yes.

Milton: The epilogue deals with something else. But the Chinaman was probably the central idea in the story originally.

Waters: Yes. The boy, the girl, the other minor characters were fictitious.

Milton: It was kind of a rough story in contrast to *People of the Valley* and *The Man Who Killed the Deer*. Did your move from Chinatown to a more or less peaceful mountain valley dictate that?

Waters: Well, I was primarily interested in the types of people in the West. *The Man Who Killed the Deer*, of course, was all Indian and *People of the Valley* were Mexican or Spanish people. But I wanted to do something on what we call in the Southwest the Coyotes, the Mestizos, the violent strain of people with mixed blood. The place where you find all these types of people is preponderantly on the Mexican border. So this was just the right locale.

Milton: Was your first move from the Mexican border to Mora?

Waters: Except for a detour to Los Angeles.

Milton: What kind of a town was Mora when you first came into it?

Waters: Well, Mora was kind of a dream town. It was in the Sangre de Cristo mountains in a beautiful little valley about half way between Las Vegas and Taos.

Milton: New Mexico.

Waters: Sure. Mora was founded by a group of seventy-six settlers from Mexico who were given a Spanish grant. It was laid out as a small town along the old Spanish-Colonial pattern. And due to the very bad roads, people living in the small remote valleys around there, it was still almost inaccessible eight months of the year. When I lived there I had a wonderful time. There were two friends of mine, Ed and Fran Tinker. Ed Tinker was a brother of the famous Major General Tinker who went down at Midway. Ed of course was kind of a black sheep younger brother. Half Osage. His wife was the daughter of a Spanish judge in Santa Fe and they were doing WPA work. We all lived in the old Mora Inn or Butler Hotel—the only three Anglos in this whole village of Spanish-speaking people. I tried my best while I was there to get the state of New Mexico, the museum, the historical society or someone to preserve this old inn as an historical site. It was built on the old Spanish style of two courtyards enclosed by rooms and separated by a *zaguan*. All the furniture for this wonderful old place had been brought from the Officers Quarters at Fort Union. Walnut-spool feather beds in every room, beautiful old hand-carved chests, marble-topped bureaus, and things like that. Wonderful bar.

23

Milton: Fort Union had been right down at the end of that same valley.

Waters: Yes. It was just about fifteen miles away.

Milton: Oh, it's that close.

Waters: So we lived there, the three of us, with Mrs. Butler who owned the place—it was later named the Butler Hotel for her. Old Mr. Butler had been a professional gambler. Run out of Oklahoma, he fled to this remote mountain valley and started this hotel, which he ran just so he could conduct gambling games. That's where he made his money. Trappers, a few traders, surveyors, and cattle-buyers would come through town, and he would get them all together for a big game at night. Being a professional gambler, he made a very good living. His wife was interesting. She had been sent to Las Vegas as a stenographer, and he had married her and brought her up there. She had lived there for years and didn't know one word of Spanish. So I asked her one time, "Mrs. Butler, how come you never learned Spanish?" "Well, it's very simple," she answered, "You know a man's brain is like a honeycomb. Once you get the little cells filled up you can't learn anything more."

Milton: At what age does this happen?

Waters: Old Butler, when I met him, was gradually going blind. He could no longer see well enough to deal but he was hiding a younger man, a half-breed Cherokee with a price on his head for killing a man. Butler taught this fellow, whom I could call Ralph, how to deal, and when the old man died Ralph took things over. He ran the hotel and carried on the gambling which kept old Mrs. Butler alive. We had a very interesting life in that old hotel.

Milton: About what year was this?

24

Waters: Oh, this was about 1935 or '36.

Milton: Somewhere in the mid-thirties. How were you making a living then?

Waters: Well, I was doing some books. I wrote *Below Grass Roots* there and was drafting *People of the Valley.* It was a quiet place to work and a cheap place to live.

Milton: Well, now, if you liked it so well, why did you finally leave there and go to Taos?

Waters: That's a complicated story. Mora was only thirty-two miles from Las Vegas, but the road was so bad it took us an hour and a half to drive the thirty-two miles, good weather, so few people came. The only time anybody came to town was on Court Day, once a month, when lawyers and judges would hold hearings and try cases in the County Court House. That's when we did most of the business in the hotel. Mrs. Butler and a Picuris Indian girl would cook the meals. I would help to make the beds. And Ralph would wait tables. One day at lunch Ralph was waiting on the table where the district attorney from Las Vegas was sitting with several lawyers and a judge. The D.A. said, "Now fellows, be very careful when you break open a biscuit that you don't get spattered with flour." Well, this made Ralph so mad he picked up a full water jug and hit the district attorney over the head, cracking open his skull. The man was rushed to the hospital and for days it was doubtful whether he would live or not. Meanwhile Ralph had fled and I had gone to Colorado Springs myself. One night, oh about midnight, I got a telephone call to go down to the railroad yards and pick up somebody. I didn't know who it was, but I didn't ask questions. I drove down to the railroad yards and there was Ralph. He was quite a sight. To get to Raton where he could hop a freight, he had given a man who owned a car a ten-dollar bill to fill the car with gas. The driver had bought a bottle of whiskey and had downed most of it before he got the gasoline and loaded Ralph in the car. During the drive they ran off the road. Ralph was thrown out of the car and through a barbed wire fence which ripped out the whole seat of his trousers and the tail end of his coat. So when he arrived in Colorado Springs after riding a freight, he was in quite bad shape. I kept him in Colorado Springs in a little tourist cottage for about three weeks listening to radio reports—the D.A. was not expected to live—there was a reward offered for information leading to Ralph's arrest. Ralph, of course, was a very nervous and high strung man and he would sit there kneading his fingers with glycerin and popping his knuckles, getting his hands in shape to deal cards. It was very distracting, as I was trying to read galley proofs on a book. Finally some friends got him a job dealing up in Silverton in the San Juan mountains. So I took him up there and left him. But to cut a very long story short, I didn't think Mora was the right place for me after that.

Milton: And still it is not far from Taos.

Waters: No. It's just thirty miles. And as I couldn't go back to Mora, I settled in Taos.

Milton: Now, the man Ralph doesn't appear as a character in any book, does he?

Waters: Not yet, but I certainly want to put him in one sometime.

Milton: Yes. The one you did pick up in *People of the Valley* is the woman Maria, who is probably one of the great female characters in American fiction. It's surprising we don't talk about her more often. Now was she an historical figure, or from your imagination, or did you meet someone as late as the 1930s who became the character?

Waters: I met Maria, who was an old woman, in the thirties. From her I got the idea for the character, but I wanted to show her whole life. For a younger woman, I used someone else. And then for her early life, I used a little girl—a homeless girl who lived with a couple of sheep herders—she was about nine years old, so I combined all three into one character.

Milton: Maria is a rather unusual woman in many ways. Were there people like this in the valley because they were isolated, so that you didn't have to invent or imagine too much to fill her out as a character?

Waters: Well, she was an awfully good character to work with while writing the thing, but I think she is quite true to life because those old Spanish families were matriarchal. My next-door neighbor now is a Spanish woman, a husky strong matriarch who dominates all Arroyo Seco. She has four sons—she dominates them all. So I think it is not unusual to have a forceful woman be boss of the whole community.

Milton: Really rather typical.

Waters: Yes.

Milton: At the same time she becomes a little exaggerated though, doesn't she? Fortune telling, the way in which she cares for the whole family—she's not just a mother. She is a kind of political leader.

Waters: Yes, a church leader, a politico, a *bruja,* etc.

Milton: So she becomes a kind of archetype-figure. Did that dam ever get built?

Waters: Just on paper. My fiction.

Milton: The fuss that was made about it in the novel served as a plot, then. Did *any* of the shenanigans ever go on that you have related in the novel as plot?

Waters: No.

Milton: So this is a kind of character study, really? In contrast to some of the other books. The Fort Union soldiers appear in this and also you mentioned the early French fur traders who had been in the valley first, and these in a sense intermingle. You have tried to pull out, have you not, a rather pure Spanish-American stream, without worrying too much about the mixtures?

Waters: That's the way they were there because they came into this isolated mountain valley and were abandoned there for a hundred years. So they became quite an inbred mountain people. I am told—I am not a linguist, but I am told—that in these remote mountain valleys the Spanish is a Cervantes Spanish, like our Tennessee hillbilly's Old English.

Milton: You work some Penitente experiences into this novel. Did you ever come into contact with some of these old time Penitentes, or ever see one of their crucifixions?

Waters: Yes. Yes I did. I went through the whole ceremony.

Milton: Went through it how? You mean you participated in it?

Waters: I was walking down the street of Mora one day. I had been living there for months. An old man shuffled up beside me, and asked, "Would you like to meet me Friday underneath the big cottonwood down the road two miles?" I said, "Yes." I didn't quite know what he meant, so I asked about it and my friends said, "Oh, Friday is Good Friday and that big tree is at the mouth of the canyon up which stands the Penitente *morada*." They made me a present to take, a bowl of sprouted wheat pudding, and I took two dollar bills tied with red yarn and went down there and I stood underneath the big cottonwood. In those days Penitente chasing wasn't the sport it is now because men with rifles would guard the canyons and the *moradas*. I waited there a long time before I finally heard the sound of the *pito,* the Penitente flute. Then I could see filing down the canyon a row of men, playing the *pito,* some of them with masks. They completely surrounded me and the tree, and then two of them stepped apart, so I got in the line. We went back to the *morada* and they went through all the ceremony. When it was over, they began the procession of death. They all filed out, picked up the huge crosses, and plodded up the canyon through the snowbanks, beating themselves with yucca whips. I was on the tail end so I could see splotches of blood on the snow banks on each side, all the way to Calvary.

Milton: They let you accompany them entirely as an observer? Quite an experience.

Waters: Oh, yes. I was very fortunate.

Three

Milton: Would you say that the Penitentes are completely taboo now?

Waters: Not now, although up until a few years ago the Penitentes were outlawed. Originally the Penitentes were organized in Italy as the Third Order of St. Francis. They spread from Italy to Spain, and were brought from Spain to Mexico, and from Mexico up to the United States.

Milton: Were they brought or were they chased?

Waters: No, it was a recognized order. These people in the remote villages throughout New Mexico adopted the order of Penitentes. And about the same time it was outlawed by the Mother Church. The people here had been left without priests for a long time so they carried on the rites themselves. Later when the church came in, it outlawed the Penitente order. Any member of the church was excommunicated if he was found to be a Penitent. I remember going swimming with boys, and they would never take off their shirts because that would reveal the scars of the lashes on their backs. But the last few years with all the new highways coming through, the church just overlooks the whole thing. Taos and Mora were the strongholds of the Penitente sect.

Milton: Did the civil government object to any of this as well as the church?

Waters: No, The civil government apparently didn't. Crucifixions were always carried on secretly up the mountain canyons so that no one could observe them.

Milton: Yes. This little town of Trampas that we went through—is there anything going on there now?

Waters: I suppose that Penitente rites are still observed there, and in Truchas too.

Milton: One doesn't hear much about them.

Waters: No. Too remote.

Milton: Onésimo, the husband of María in *People of the Valley,* actually dies from the crucifixion. But I think you suggested the intent, except for the whippings of the crucifixion, was symbolic rather than actual.

Waters: It was a symbolic thing. The trouble is that the selected Cristos had to carry a huge cross up a mountain canyon several miles, sometimes through deep snow. It overtaxed their strength and being bound on the cross was a worse ordeal. Often they would die before they could be taken down. It wasn't too unusual for a man to die.

Milton: This didn't stop them, however.

Waters: No.

Milton: María—*People of the Valley*—was kind of an adviser to the people with her reading of goat skulls. Is this a genuine super-stition of the valley again, and would that be Spanish rather than Indian? Or do you recall where you picked up the astrological readings of bone skulls?

Waters: Apparently it was an old custom practiced throughout the Southwest and Mexico. I'll tell you where you can find some more about it, in Frank Dobie. Dobie writes about it in several passages and we talked about it several times.

Milton: Probably goat skulls because they had a lot of goats in the mountains. Do any of these superstitions remain in the Mora area?

Waters: Well, when I was over there in the thirties, they certainly did. Whether they do now or not, I don't know.

Milton: Now in Taos, we know that this has become kind of a tourist town many months of the year at least. Right outside is the pueblo which was the basis for your novel, *The Man Who Killed the Deer.* One has the feeling at least that the customs and traditions have been maintained quite carefully. How did you get well enough acquainted with the Pueblo Indians to gain material for that novel?

Waters: Well, after having lived there for twenty or twenty-five years with those people, one gradually soaks in quite a bit. You can't ask an Indian a direct question about his ceremonies, because they won't answer, but if you know them, one will tell you something, and someone else will tell you something else, and you can gradually put it all together and arrive at something.

Milton: This happened because you had been a friend rather than truly a writer? What about a professional writer coming into the pueblo, would he get as much?

Waters: Oh, I don't think if you went to an Indian with a notebook in hand and began to ask questions that you would ever get anything. Most ethnologists and anthropologists who come to make studies select certain Indians they call informants, paying them so much an hour, but you can never be sure of the stuff they write. The Indians lie about half the time, but being told little by little over a long period of years you can be sure that the information is correct.

Milton: I met a man named Frank there a year or two ago who lived on the south side of the stream. Do you happen to know him?

Waters: I have a very dear friend of some twenty-five years named Frank, and he, as a matter of fact, was once arrested for killing a deer out of season. That was the incident that started *The Man Who Killed the Deer.* I did not know Frank at the time. I just happened to be in the Court House when his trial came up and it gave me the idea for the book, but a few years later I happened to get acquainted with him. He has worked for me and been a friend for many years. He comes up to the ranch often, and has always shoed the horses, done chores, and helped with building, but in the twenty-five years that I have known him, we have never discussed this incident or the book. I am sure he knows about it.

Milton: He must.

Waters: We just don't talk about it.

Milton: He was there last summer and I met him.

Waters: He was there, yes, you met him. He's a very fine man, but, like most of the older Indians, he doesn't like to talk about these things. So we just don't talk.

Milton: Then you got none of your material from him?

Waters: No, I got none of it from him.

Milton: What year did that incident occur, do you recall?

Waters: I'd say in the late thirties.

Milton: Now the particular problem which you dealt with in that novel, could that still happen now or was this—oh, that's only twenty, twenty-five years ago—is that far enough back to make a difference?

Waters: The problem, the background theme of the book, is the fight of the Taos Indians for their sacred area in the mountains around Blue Lake. The issue came up in the thirties before Congress which granted the Indians a fifty-year tenure on the area for religious purposes. Since then, tourists have packed into the area, dirtied up the lake and so on. Now the Indians are pressing for a clear title to the area, beginning the whole controversy again. The

Anglos in Taos, politicians, and several newspapers are claiming that the Indians are trying to gain control of the watershed and grab land in the public domain, although the land always has been legally theirs. The issue is a hot potato, a national controversy that will probably involve the Court of Indian Claims, both houses of Congress, and maybe the Supreme Court before it's settled.*

Milton: If the Indians get Blue Lake, they would presumably get a wide strip coming down alongside the Taos stream also.

Waters: About fifty thousand acres are involved. The Forest Service reserved the right to patrol that area in case of fire, to stop overgrazing, and prevent flood hazards. But it hasn't stopped the tourists packing in there.

Milton: Who is the authority in the pueblo today? They have their own, I understand, quite separate from the Federal government and town authorities.

Waters: The pueblo has its own government. They have a governor and a council to make their own local laws, and that privilege was given them by President Lincoln. He gave the governor of every pueblo a little gold-handled cane which signified their right to exercise jurisdiction over their own local affairs. So the old governor on all state occasions, wrapped in his blanket, carries this Lincoln cane as a mark of his office. Yet, at the same time, national supervision is exercised through the Indian Bureau.

Milton: They have a war chief too, don't they, under the governor?

Waters: A Fiscal who attends to affairs with the visiting Spanish priest. The war chief deals with affairs outside the pueblo. And the old cacique who tends to all religious matters, as the governor tends to all secular affairs.

*The land around their sacred Blue Lake was restored to the Indians of Taos Pueblo by Congress in December, 1970. It is quite likely that *The Man Who Killed the Deer* played a part in the long fight for Blue Lake.

Milton: The war chief runs their farms then? They do some farming off the pueblo.

Waters: You see, it means cleaning the ditches—you see, it is all communal so every man has to devote several days' work cleaning out the ditches and doing other communal duties.

Milton: They maintain, I know, rather strong prejudices against plumbing, electric lights, and what have you, in the pueblos.

Waters: Well, yes, there is a schism among them as there is among us—the liberals and the conservatives. The younger men who have been away to the army, had their hair cut, want plumbing, electricity, water, and all the conveniences, but the older men will not let telephones and electricity in. It's the battle between the old men and the young men.

Milton: Yes, and this is likely to change when the young men become older.

Waters: The older men are dying out. It won't be too long before the pueblo will be modernized, I am sure.

Milton: Is it true that the older people in each family live on the ground floor in the pueblo and the young ones up in the fourth and fifth stories, climbing the ladders?

Waters: I doubt if that's true because more and more families are building little summer houses away from the pueblo.

Milton: In the mountains?

Waters: Yes, they live in these little summer homes except during the winter. Then they come in and live in their little cramped apartments.

Milton: How strong is the use of the kiva yet? Recently we were kept from going around behind where I had been several times

36

before, as if something were going on. Does this custom run on down through the young people too? The use of the kiva?

Waters: Yes, the kiva is closed.

Milton: What experiences have you had with kiva practices?

Waters: That's something I would rather not get into.

Milton: O.K. Now with Martiniano in *The Man Who Killed the Deer* there is a sense of justice expressed that works two ways. First, you have the Indian against the white man's court, but, within the pueblo itself, there are mixed feelings about Martiniano. On what basis is this best explained?

Waters: I think Martiniano could be looked at now just as a young G.I.—he does not want to conform to Pueblo customs. Of course, the old men are hellbent to make him conform—in other words, go back to the blanket. A young boy who has been to Germany, Korea, Europe, he wants something else.

Milton: Yes. He has simply lost some of the old traditions. And because of their age differences the people in the pueblo would be split in their attitudes toward him. The old trader in that novel, does he come from anyone you have met?

Waters: Yes, he was a very fine man. Just wonderful. You have been to Taos and know the building where Frenchy's restaurant, La Doña Luz, is and the Book Shop. Well, that was Ralph's home. The big dining room was Ralph's private dining room. The Book Shop was his trading post, and the kitchen is where he had his Indian craftsmen. He was the old type of trader, a profane but lovable man, who didn't give a damn about selling knick-knacks to tourists for fifty cents or a dollar. He was only interested in going out, as he had for forty years, to collect the finest things—beaded buckskin, rare fetishes, good silver—to sell to museums like the Heye Indian Museum in New York, and to private collectors. It used to annoy him when tourists would come in and want to spend a dollar. He would curse them and run them out. But a wonderful old man.

Milton: He was one, then, who had a love of artifacts and for materials of the land.

Waters: He sure did. He had been a trader all his life. He sold all over the country and made out very well.

Milton: Do you have any idea where he came from? It is always striking to the person who, on the first visit to Taos, sees the mixture of people; of course, it is a tri-lingual community.

Waters: He came from Denver. His name was Ralph Myers. I believe he had a German background, one of the old German traders. In the early days we had a lot of Frenchmen like Ceran St. Vrain in Taos. Also some fine old Germans, the Scheurichs and Gusdorfs.

Milton: I have seen those old names in the cemetery there. The Indians still, of course, come into town quite a bit with their blankets wrapped around them. I got a little bit disgusted one time—I forget his name now—with the fellow who has the motel at the south end of town, where they have the Indian dances at night.

Waters: Oh, Jack Denver.

Milton: Yes, he seems to be exploiting them. Do you have any idea what the attitude of the Pueblo Indian is toward that kind of thing?

Waters: Oh, they just dress up in their fancy duds, the feathers and war bonnets, and probably get a dollar or so apiece for doing it for half an hour.

Milton: Yes, they are just in it for the money. Can you think of one characteristic more than any other—this is a problem that has worried me in confronting some of the Pueblos down there—a characteristic in a visitor that would allow him to get close to the Indians? What do they like in people?

Waters: Oh, I think people are the same the world over. If you have a sense of what they call *simpatia* or *simpatico*—sympathy—just friendly, and don't ask too many questions, you could make friends there very nicely.

Milton: You have written in several places among your novels of incidents of white men among Indians. I think Ona's husband—what was his name? Jonathan Cable?—he goes out to visit them, simply sits by the fire, makes no overtures and just waits. Is this the attitude you are describing?

Waters: I guess so.

Milton: Do you still go over to the pueblo?

Waters: Yes, I have a lot of friends—I ride there quite often. I like the feeling.

Milton: You have never discussed with Martiniano that incident. Have any of these people talked to you about your books? Do they hear about them at all? Or is this out of their context altogether?

Waters: Well, when I wrote the book I was afraid that every friend of mine would be punished severely for having told me some information, because a noted woman ethnologist had come out and made a study of Taos Pueblo. It was printed as an ethnological paper, and the Indians found out about it. Every person that talked to her as an informant was brought before the council and several were fined or whipped, so I was afraid that would happen to all my friends. I happened to be in California at the time I received the first advance copy of the book, so I sent it back to the council's interpreter and requested him to show it to the council, to read passages. And if there were any objections to wire me and I would come right back before the council. As a result I did not have any repercussions at all.

Milton: No repercussions at all? No one has talked to you about it either?

Waters: I have had people in the years since come up and say, "Gee, you told us a lot of very fine things we didn't know." That is, younger people who haven't had any advantages of kiva training. G.I.'s who have been away, you know. They appreciated it, which is what I liked, you see. The older people will die out and it will all die out and this is on record for their children.

Milton: Do you actually look forward to the pueblo disappearing in about a hundred years or so? Seems strange, because it has been there for quite a few centuries now.

Waters: Probably since 1200.

Milton: Will it survive the kind of progress we see going on now?

Waters: No. The land is owned communally. It is not owned by individuals with fee simple titles, so they can never mortgage or sell it. But what will happen when the old people die off and the young people want to get out in the white world? That will be a problem. I think it ought to be preserved together with all the other old pueblos as a wonderful example of prehistoric architecture in this country.

Milton: We mentioned a kind of practical problem earlier that comes in here too. María in *People of the Valley* says or thinks something at the end of the novel about fulfillment rather than progress. It is a nice distinction, but now, do you see any hope of this carrying over to the white race?

Waters: Values will carry over, maybe not in the same medium. The ceremonies themselves will be given up but the meanings and values I hope will be carried over.

Milton: But they will almost have to seep out of context, won't they? Rather than remain dominant in the pueblo?

Waters: I think so. Yes.

Milton: Well, could you give just one instance of how this might work? You know when you talk about values you are on slippery ground. What is a value? How is it preserved? Can you think of one value within the pueblo to be maintained outside the pueblo?

Waters: Well, this would be getting into it, but for example: C.G. Jung, the great Swiss psychologist, visited Taos Pueblo many years ago and he found in several Indian myths the same archetypal dominants and meanings expressed by the unconscious in his own patients. Navaho and Pueblo sandpaintings in design and structure are mandalas also—archetypal symbols found over all the world. So all humanity carries the same universal values but expresses them in different racial mediums. The mediums will change and disappear, but the values will endure.

Milton: You think now that this is confined to the West? I have said on occasion that I think Eastern fiction is influenced by Freud, but Western fiction has certain affinities with the Jungian principles. Would you agree with that?

Waters: Oh, certainly. I think Freud is old-fashioned. He was the great innovator, the pioneer, but psychology has gone far beyond him. Jung has advanced further, into a deeper level. What he calls the collective unconscious embraces all the values we have preserved since we were primitives.

Milton: We are not going to be one bit willing to go back to primitive living conditions.

Waters: No, but the inherent—

Milton: The problem is to separate progress from fulfillment.

Waters: And to carry over valid primitive values into modern living.

Milton: Now, again, even though we generally agree that fiction shouldn't get at teaching of this sort, do you see anything in *The Man Who Killed the Deer* or *People of the Valley* which you know, in literature, would make this kind of contribution?

Waters: Well, all I know is that you can't put these things into words because then you preach—you are no longer telling a story. In *The Man Who Killed the Deer* I tried to do that by simply putting these unspoken values into words printed in italics. Because Indians don't talk like this, they don't put it into words. So I just put it into italics—to separate it from the story-telling context of the novel, and still give the emotional value. My way of solving a technical problem.

Milton: This makes *The Man Who Killed the Deer* a little different from *People of the Valley,* which is completely an imagistic novel, and allows whatever information or values there are to come out of the images.

Waters: These Spanish people were down-to-earth people. But Indians, as I mentioned earlier, have this mystical overtone; it is difficult to get.

Milton: You mean difficult to get as an artist presenting the images for people to understand.

Four

Milton: *People of the Valley* reaches some kind of a conclusion toward the end of the novel when Maria feels something concerning these images that suggests a view of art that probably you are involved in. I would like to read one passage to lead us into a discussion of perhaps the Indian way of getting at the values of the earth. This is when María was a very old woman, along toward the end of her life. You described very carefully her dirty black reboso, streaked and rusty as oxidized iron in the rock; she wiggled a bare toe in the green grass; a beetle crawled across her leg and the robin chirped. These are very insignificant details in themselves, but, put together, it was these she really felt and answered. "Men pass on and their shadows follow, but the heaving earth and its blind vitality remain changeless and indestructible." Now this is a kind of celebration rather than an attempt to understand it rationally, and I think what interests us among the rituals of the Indians is whether this is not the same process they go through in their various ceremonials when they are not taking images and using them to celebrate the earth. Now for the studies you have done for *Masked Gods* and *Book of the Hopi,* what, by and large, has come up in connection with ceremonialism that could serve as a generalization of it?

Waters: Maybe it's our conception of images. These you have read may have been the author's images while trying to characterize this woman in terms of the earth of which she is an archetypal image really. Whereas, in Indian ceremonialism the images are abstract symbols in most cases: they are not exact things, but abstract images. Now without getting into a long harangue, most people don't know what an Indian ceremony is except that the Indians pray and sing and dance, but I might just briefly comment on the Hopi ceremonies. There are nine ceremonies in the annual cycle. The first comes in the fall, has many rituals, and lasts for nine days and nights. It symbolizes the dawn of creation when the seeds of human life are planted, which is a literary image. It takes us up just as if the whole earth was at the dawn of creation, so they go through the rituals of planting the seeds of life. Then about Christmas time, the second one comes in, and this portrays the germination and the sprouting of these forms of life. In the third ceremony, man appears, and they erect houses for the first time. Now all these are in abstract symbols, but this is what they represent. The second group of three ceremonies comes in the summer when the life they have planted comes to full maturity, like the corn. Then the third set of three ceremonies follows in the fall and that has to do with harvesting, getting ready for the cycle to be repeated. So what they are telling in abstract ritualism is the creation myth, the book of Genesis which is repeated every year. The creation of the world did not happen just once, but it happens every year, and it is continually repeated. So these are simple things, but it is their abstract quality that makes them so—you might say—unintelligible to people who don't know their symbolism.

Milton: In the first part of this cycle of creation are there rather close relationships to the book of Genesis, to the Christian myth? Are there floods, for example?

Waters: It may seem strange to us that the Hopi creation myth holds that people have lived in three preceding worlds before this one. In each world, mankind was destroyed by a cataclysm except for a few people saved to be transplanted to the next. The same belief in four preceding worlds is expressed by the creation myths of the Mayas in Yucatan and Guatemala, by the Aztecs in Mexico, and it is the same as held by Tibetan and ancient Chinese mystics. Now these previous worlds are not to be accepted literally as we accept the Garden of Eden. Because this is ostensibly a parable. I don't think either that most of us believe there were an actual Adam and Eve and a serpent and an apple as related in our own Christian creation myth. These four worlds of the Aztecs, the Toltecs, the Mayas and the Tibetans represent stages of evolution mankind has gone through during many eons. So that is what links these ceremonies of so-called savage, ignorant Indians to modern psychology and to other world religions.

Milton: Is there a serpent image or symbol in the Hopi religion?

Waters: The principal Aztec deity was called Quetzalcoatl. The name is derived from two words, the "quetzal" bird and the serpent "coatl." Hence this feathered serpent is an abstract symbol which links heaven and earth as represented by the bird and the snake combined. In short, the hermetic meaning of Quetzalcoatl is the reconciliation of spirit and matter. Now as the Hopis are part of the Uto-Aztecan language family they may be a remnant of the ancient Toltec-Aztec-Mayan complex. Because they also have the symbolism—they also have the serpent. Probably the best example is the famous Hopi snake dance where the Hopis actually dance with live rattlesnakes and bullsnakes in their mouths.

Milton: Then the symbol of the snake actually becomes a literal thing within the ceremony.

Waters: That's right, literal and archetypal.

Milton: So, in some respects, these ceremonies are to the Hopis perhaps what our literature is to us, and this is why they keep repeating it.

Waters: They repeat it because they act it out. They don't sit down and read these things, but they act it out. It's a living thing in which they all participate, which makes it a live, meaningful thing.

Milton: Why, precisely, might they not do this other than as a ritual? That is, we come to the question: Why ritual at all? As far as you know, are they still trying to appease nature, or are they trying to get at a mystery? Or has this become simply an art form?

Waters: No, it's not a Sunday religion like ours. It's a religious experience. In other words, they really live through these great ceremonies all year long.

Milton: And they expect to come out of each one psychologically changed in some way.

Waters: Psychologically, they do benefit greatly.

Milton: Now, when you were writing or doing research for the *Book of the Hopi,* you lived on the reservation in Arizona for six months?

Waters: I lived out in the Hopi country for the best part of three years while I was doing the book. We had about thirty old Hopis who would tell us the esoteric meanings of the rituals—tell us in Hopi to take down on a tape recorder. That's the way I did it, and these tapes are now kept on permanent file. When the people pass away—these older men—their children's children will have a record of what their forefathers actually believed.

Milton: Was there any way of telling how authentic these stories were, or have they, as far as you can tell, been watered down, or are the experiences still there?

Waters: Cross-checking and personal observation assure me they are real, quite wonderful things. If these ceremonies were given, like the Passion Play of Oberammergau, in Europe, tens of thousands of Americans would make pilgrimages to Europe to see them, but because they are given here people pay no attention to them.

Milton: Would they be allowed to watch many of these things if they wanted to?

Waters: Most of the rituals take place in the kiva and you can't witness them. The last day, the public ceremony is held in the plaza and everyone is invited. Those are colorful things. I remember two years ago we went to the midwinter ceremony of Pachavu, the bean planting ceremony. You know what a kachina is.

Milton: Yes.

Waters: Anthropomorphic figures, and I suppose there were one hundred fifty kachinas, each wearing different costumes, all uttering their own strange cries, etc., all coming in to the snowy plaza and dancing all afternoon. It was a gorgeous spectacle. There is just nothing like it in this country.

Milton: Now is this something that only the men take part in? Where do the women and children fit into these general ceremonies?

Waters: There are women in most ceremonies, but their parts are usually played by men. Men who wear women's costumes.

Milton: Do you suspect that this has anything at all to do with our old Christian conception of Adam and Eve? Eve being the one who grabbed the apple and therefore is being outlawed from that point on? Talking about the instinctual, that seems to be paralleled in many religions.

Waters: Of course in the fall ceremonies the women take part. Because the fall ceremony is held in the harvest time, getting ready for the germination again, and so it has a sexual significance, the seed to begin a new cycle, so women do take part.

Milton: That might also then be because the women serve as laborers and do the harvesting.

Waters: The men do most of the work in the fields, but of course the women sometimes help.

Milton: At least this comes out of our traditional view of the Indian.

Waters: But these are very great ceremonies—they are really mystery plays in the old tradition of the mystery plays of Europe. And they are quite wonderful.

Milton: Yes. And we have been discussing this over and over. Briefly, is there anything that a different culture and a different race can pull out of these ceremonies to use or benefit from in some way? Now you were attempting, I believe, to get at a kind of practical application for the Hopi. This is a puzzling thing to most people.

Waters: It's puzzling to everyone because we know that this Indian business is probably going to pass out of existence. The young men aren't being immured in the kiva and aren't being taught all these things. Probably within a generation most of these ceremonies will be given up. The big question is: Will the values which they represent be carried over and expressed in a different medium, or be lost?

Milton: If they were expressed differently, would we simply get back to, say, our Christian telling of the same stories? This is what I am wondering—can the Hopi stories survive without blending into the others?

Waters: Can the Christian religion survive its literal myth?

Milton: Well, we have been seeing some of this.

Waters: In other words, if we no longer believe in Adam and Eve literally and that there was a Noah's Ark, does this destroy the base of Christian religion or will those values be carried over, when we recognize them as parables? Theirs is a comparable problem.

Milton: Yes, a matter of retaining certain instincts.

Waters: Basic archetypal images I call them.

Milton: Now you mention that Dr. Jung had come to New Mexico and that in his books there are at least a few pages recording his visit. Was it among Indians or did he simply go through the state, do you remember?

Waters: Yes, in his autobiography, *Memories, Dreams and Reflections,* he relates a visit he made to Taos Pueblo, saying that these people were really quite pure in spirit, that is, not moralistic purity, but they still held on to the intuitional values more than we do. He also expressed a great admiration for the symbols and designs of the sandpaintings which were equivalent to mandalas found throughout all the world since prehistoric times. His patients who were recovering would also draw variations of these same mandalas which are symbols of psychic wholeness.

Milton: How are the sandpaintings used? We've seen pictures of them, we see them finished and undisturbed, but aren't they broken up frequently?

Waters: Well, Navaho sandpaintings are made on the floor of the hogan or hut where the ceremony is held by simply carrying in different colored natural sands and designs, all peculiar designs to us—symbols. Then the medicine man or singer seats himself at the head with the patient squatting on the sandpainting and goes through the ritual of healing his ill patient. The patient may have a real bodily illness or he may have been a boy that went away to war and killed, and needs a restorative—a healing ceremony to take away the guilt of murder. So it could be either physical or mental, psychosomatic as we say. At the conclusion of the ceremony, the singer takes the sand from the sandpainting and sprinkles it over the patient's body, and this wonderful sandpainting, of course, is then destroyed. It is not made primarily as an art form, but rather for this specific purpose.

Milton: In that case, then, he doesn't pick up sand haphazardly, he takes it from out of the design according to some kind of pattern. Do you know enough about that to—

Waters: Well, they are all equated—all sandpaintings are equated to the directions, north, south, east, and west, and all these directions have a symbolic color—blue to the south, black to the north, yellow to the west and white to the east. There are gods or psychic forces in each direction and these correspond with parts of the human body, so as the singer destroys it, he picks up from the sandpainting those corresponding directional parts of the painting.

Milton: Would any special designs be worked out in the middle of the painting according to the mental problem or the physical disease of the patient?

Waters: No, they're not composed spontaneously for each patient. Each Chant or Way, as the ceremony is known, has a traditional set of sandpaintings as well as a corresponding myth, songs, and prayers.

Milton: That would correspond—

Waters: Yes, sir. There are many, many designs. Oh, I suppose one ceremony will have from eight to twelve different sandpaintings.

Milton: So then the patient and doctor move along side by side.

Waters: Yes, ah ha!

Milton: What about the figure of the Ye-bet-chai? Is this a kind of high priestly function?

Waters: Yes, Ye-bet-chai is the grandfather of the gods, the leading character of the pantheon you might say.

Milton: For a special kind of ceremony?

Waters: Yes.

Milton: Other than the creation—

Waters: No. The correct name for the ceremony differs—the Night-Chant, the Mountain Chant, etc.

Milton: What are their special functions? Is there any kind of hierarchy? This is what I am trying to get at: Within these ceremonies is there one which corresponds to High Mass in the Catholic Church?

Waters: No.

Milton: There is no distinction?

Waters: Each ceremony is held for a certain illness—mental or physical—so they have a ceremony to fit the trouble.

Milton: Does this carry over into the rugs which they weave?

Waters: Yes. These so-called Ye-bet-chai rugs are simply copies of some of the sandpaintings. The Navahos just started weaving them a few years ago.

Milton: They weren't substitutes for the sandpaintings?

Waters: Oh, no.

Milton: So again, we are back to a kind of art form, some way of preserving the designs. I have heard that a Ye-bet-chai rug is not supposed to be walked on. Is this true?

Waters: It is not a true rug. Originally it was a blanket and parts of it are left out. Because of the whole design—all the full symbolism in the sandpainting—something is left out.*

Milton: Now, the materials in the *Book of the Hopi* do not overlap entirely those in the *Masked Gods,* do they?

Waters: No. *Masked Gods* is a study of Navaho and Pueblo ceremonialism in general outline and meaning, where the *Book of the Hopi* is only Hopi ceremonialism itself.

Milton: How are the various tribes, as I guess we would call them, related? We talked about Pueblos in connection with *The Man Who Killed the Deer,* and Navaho and Hopi in two non-fiction books. Are these people essentially the same or are these people—?

Waters: Well, we don't know where the Pueblos came from. They were here as early primitives shortly after the birth of Christ. The Navahos were a Mongolian people who arrived here very late. They probably arrived here in the Southwest where they are now as late as 1600. Just after the Spanish got here. The first Spanish explorers in the Southwest made no reference to the Navahos at all. But some years later when the newer arrivals came in they began reporting statistics on the Navahos. So they are comparatively late arrivals and they borrowed a great deal from the Pueblos—they learned to weave and plant corn, they learned sandpainting from the Pueblos.

Milton: I suppose the important thing out of all this is—what has your study of ceremonialism or your study of the characteristics of

*Sandpaintings were made for healing ceremonies. They varied according to the nature of the ailment and the skill of the artist. After the patient had sat on the sandpainting, it was destroyed at the end of the day. No copies were made. Because of that and also because sandpainting designs in paintings and in rugs are not used for healing, the latter designs are always incomplete.

the Indian tribes and so forth, their beliefs, their religions—what has this done for you personally in your own confrontation?

Waters: Well, I have often wondered, and everybody asks, "Why do you write so much about Indians?" I can answer only that I have lived with Indians all of my life and they interest me. And I probably justify it rationally by saying that, after all, we are all interested in our relationship to our own land, to our own earth, and the Indians are indigenous to this continent. The Indian is much different from our European white, so I think that we have a great deal to learn from their expression of it in their own idiom.

Milton: Do you think that if you moved out of New Mexico—this is a theoretical question—and were maybe plunked down in Vermont or Ohio or someplace, would you have any reason then for retaining the beliefs of these people?

Waters: Oh, I think once you accept Christianity, the belief in Christianity, the mere fact that you live in Africa doesn't destroy those values.

Milton: We keep getting back to these values that we don't get pinned down very well. This I think is part of the difficulty. What actually would you retain, if you moved to Ohio?

Waters: Well, what I mean by values—if I find correspondences between Indian ceremonialism and psychology and Oriental religious philosophies, these are basic values.

Milton: Would this actually affect your behavior? It is one thing to live with or next to the Indians and behave as they do, and this is very comfortable, but if you were taken out of that situation, could you pull their values with you—?

Waters: Oh, I think we live by our own values, and if any religion gives you values of life, I think you retain them, even though you don't live literally by the Indian's.

Milton: Just like an Indian in downtown New York?

Waters: Oh, yes. You don't have to beat a drum and all those things to be an Indian.

Milton: No, no. But primarily what would you become? This is what we keep driving after. Would you simply let your neighbor alone and live with some kind of taciturnity as the Indian does?

Waters: No, I don't think we should confuse the outward way of life of the white and the Indian with the inner life. To be an Indian you don't have to grow your own corn and eat coarse ground meal. You can be a vice president of the United States, you know.

Milton: So what it comes down to then is that this is an individual inner matter.

Five

Milton: The painters who live in and around Taos don't consider themselves regional in that respect do they?

Waters: They don't, but a lot of people do. The Hudson River School, the Taos School, etc. But I don't think they do any more than Carmel or La Jolla painters consider themselves Pacific Coast artists.

Milton: Wouldn't there be an even greater objection if these painters in Taos painted scenes that they had seen maybe twenty or thirty years earlier? Then there would be no point in being in Taos, would there? How many galleries are there now? Within the town?

Waters: I would say between twenty-five and thirty.

Milton: And they all manage reasonably well to stay in business—

Waters: They all do and do well. As a matter of fact, the *Wall Street Journal* several years ago reported that more paintings were sold in Taos than in any other city in the United States outside of New York City.

Milton: And that has to take place mostly in the summer months too.

Waters: Two hundred forty thousand dollars worth of paintings a year, I've heard.

Milton: You have done a book on one of the painters who has lived there, Leon Gaspard. So I take it you knew him very well and some of the reasons why he settled in Taos.

Waters: Yes. There were two very fine artists whose lives were so parallel, it was very strange. They were both born in Russia. The first one was Nicolai Fechin who was born in Kazan and was picked out as a young boy of ten for his extraordinary talent in carving wood by scouts of the Imperial Art Academy under the Czar. He was taken to the Imperial Art Academy in Petrograd to undergo a thorough course of training for seventeen years before he was allowed to show a painting, and call himself an artist. I think that's a good commentary on some of our young people who spend a summer at the Art Students League in New York, and then put on a beret and call themselves artists. Fechin finally was given a great showing of his work in the International Glass Palace in Munich, Germany. His showing created quite a sensation. It was taken to Paris and London and all around Europe. But he was a very simple peasant-type man who hated big cities. So he fled back to Kazan and became a director in an art museum there for the government until the Bolshevik Revolution began. Then he hid out in a cabin with his wife and child and a cow along the Volga River deep in the forest. He was able to eke out an existence until the Red Cross of America discovered he and his family and brought them to New York City. Fechin eventually arrived in Taos where he built a home and a studio. All the woodwork he carved and hand-rubbed himself—it was a Russian style house—a very beautiful place. Fechin was of Tartar stock. As a boy he used to visit across the Volga River with these wild Tartar tribes. Well, in Taos he found the same terms of appeal because the Indians were comparable to the Tartar tribes in Russia and our Spanish-speaking people similar to the Russian *muziks* or peasants. He was primarily a portrait painter and a great colorist and did some of his finest work here. Unfortunately there was a divorce in the family and he fled and went down to Mexico, then over to the island of Bali and Java, and to Japan. He died a few years ago, but his

56

paintings are now selling for thousands of dollars apiece and they are very difficult to obtain. Russia, I understand, is trying to obtain all the paintings they can for a great show in Russia. Fechin is an internationally famous artist, a great painter.

Milton: Is he the one you talked about in your book on the Colorado River?

Waters: Yes. He was very kind. He did four charcoal sketches to illustrate *The Colorado* for me and also a very fine color painting of a Pueblo dance for the book's cover jacket.

Milton: Do you have those original sketches?

Waters: Yes, I do. They are certainly treasures. It's strange that a little town like Taos, New Mexico would get two artists from Russia. Entirely different too, yet with parallel backgrounds. The other artist was named Leon Gaspard. It's a French name because his grandfather emigrated from France to Russia, where he traded for furs and fine rugs in the Siberian steppes. As a young boy Leon used to accompany his father on these trading expeditions to the Kirgiz and Kazakh tribes. At the age of between nineteen and twenty he finally made it to Paris. He arrived there about 1899 or 1900, the great era of modern art, the days of real Bohemianism. He studied there for ten or twelve years and became a fine professional painter. When war broke out, he enlisted as an aerial observer in the French Army, and was shot down in a plane, but survived. He then came to the United States and went to several places including Provincetown to find a quiet place to paint.

Milton: The Taos of the East.

Waters: And finally arrived in Taos. He lived there for four years, taking time out, however, to make a trip to China. He loved Peking. It was a wonderful city to paint, he always said. And in 1929 he made a horseback trip from Peking, China across Inner

Mongolia and Outer Mongolia to the mountains of Tibet and then back through Chinese Turkestan—and most of this on horseback. Took him about two years. During that time he carried bolts of very fine Chinese silk, light in weight and a good texture to work on. Then he came back to Taos. You probably know his home. It's a great Byzantine-style house.

Milton: Yes.

Waters: And has lived there, painting. So here were these two Russians, both world travelers, both colorists with a strange Asiatic color sense. However, one was primarily a portrait painter and the other a genre painter. Well, this book that I have done is a monograph on Gaspard, whom I knew for twenty-five years. It has full page, full color reproductions of paintings done in Mongolia, in China, and also of the Navahos and the Pueblos. He felt just as much at home in a Navaho hogan as he did in the *yurts* or huts of the Mongolian tribesmen. The text is very simple, illustrated with a great number of his fabulous travel stories.

Milton: Now do you think that he, being more than just a cosmopolitan man, found again this rather close relationship between the Oriental ways of living and those of the Indians in New Mexico? Is there more than a simple accident to his settling in Taos?

Waters: He could find very little difference, especially in the nineteen-twenties and thirties when he would go out on the Navaho reservation. The Mongolians were nomads like the Navahos—they travelled around with their herds of mares, living on mare's milk and on goats. The Navahos were also semi-nomadic, following their sheep. Gaspard found a great similarity not only between their ways of life, but their physical structure and some of the Navaho words, and felt right at home. He was not interested in ethnology, of course, but each Navaho child is born with what they call the Mongolian spot at the base of the spine. It's a round blue spot about the size of a silver dollar, but disappears about a couple of weeks after birth. There is no doubt that the Navahos were of Mongolian origin. Gaspard found the people very similar.

Milton: What about the nature of the land itself? We hear that many painters go to Taos simply because of the purity of the colors, coming out of the peculiar atmosphere at that altitude.

Waters: Well, the high dry air, from a mile to ten thousand feet high, and the arid desert, it makes for a brilliant turquoise sky above beautiful colored earth. Those red and salmon-colored buttes, white limestone cliffs, it's a beautiful place to paint. And the Navaho women's gingham skirts and velveteen blouses, and their blankets are very highly colored too. Gaspard found the same color in Mongolia. The Mongolian steppes, he told me, were covered with "gobi"—it looked to him like a very hard gravel which reflected the blue of the sky. The Chinese called it "The Land of the Blue Sky." But it was due to that bright clarity of the atmosphere that he could paint so well; everything took color immediately.

Milton: Have you considered Gaspard to be one of the major painters who lived in Taos?

Waters: Yes, I think Fechin and Leon Gaspard were two of the outstanding painters.

Milton: But of the many who are still working there, which ones do you know quite well, and think highly of?

Waters: Well, there is one painter entirely different—a very fine man whose name will always live in art—his name is Andrew Dasburg. Andrew Dasburg was born in Paris and was one of the innovators of modern art. He does abstract paintings, and was given, two years ago, a traveling retrospective show that went all over the United States, sponsored by the Ford Foundation. He is still living in Taos and doing very fine work.

Milton: Periodically there have been little arguments in the Taos newspaper between the abstractionists and the literalists, depending upon which critic praises them.

Waters: Well, there is always that old battle between the modernists and the realists, but Taos is full of painters and dabblers of every kind. It's been an art center since 1900. It is like Provincetown or Carmel or Laguna Beach.

Milton: This raises a question I think you brought up, I think it was in *Below Grass Roots*—the materials themselves in the West. When you have a landscape as large as, say, that of New Mexico, the artist, whether he be a writer or a painter, has some difficulty in putting a frame around it because it's so terribly large. Now do you see that this has something to do with a distinction between objective and abstract painting? Would one tend to go in one direction or the other to achieve this kind of frame?

Waters: I don't know. It seems to me that some of these new painters are doing an excellent job because they are primarily concerned with the design and balance and juxtaposition of planes—vertical cliffs rising out of a horizontal flat desert, the strata, the way they are tilted, etc.

Milton: That's what I was wondering. As the camera takes a scene literally, it has a good deal of difficulty in encompassing the broad landscape, and I am wondering if abstraction in literature wouldn't be a normal outcome also.

Waters: Painters are strange birds. I always liked one thing Gaspard said: "Subject makes no difference at all. When I look at something, I look at it first in terms of color. Do I have a nice pleasing color scheme that's broken by an outstanding color dominant?" But some of these abstract painters are interested in design; they are like sculptors, they look at the balance, at the structure of the planes. The same with Fechin. He preferred to paint old peasant people with wrinkles in their faces. Whereas a writer looks for drama, not in terms of color or plane structure, but drama in characterization.

Milton: Dorothy Brett is still living in Taos and still painting. Do you know her quite well?

Waters: Yes. I know Brett—came from England. She studied in Slade School, was the daughter of Lord Escher, and followed the D.H. Lawrences to Taos. Well, she's an entirely different painter. You can't compare her with anyone. She lives out of town on the edge of the reservation and she paints Indians in a mystical, decorative style of her own. Very, very fine pictures. For years she has been concentrating on doing huge canvases of Indian ceremonials, and they are very expensive and are bought by museums for permanent showing. They are extraordinary paintings. She also does a lot of very charming things, which she calls her pot-boilers, which I think are just as original and remarkable.

Milton: Would you say that her painting has been made somewhat more effective by her relationship with Lawrence?

Waters: No. Her painting stands on its own. She is the only painter I know who has caught on canvas the inherent mystical strain of Indians.

Milton: Now what about Lawrence's own paintings? There are a few of them still in Taos, aren't there?

Waters: Well—I don't like them. I just can't stand them! His whole collection of paintings has been taken over by Saki Karavas, who owns the La Fonda Hotel in Taos. He has one room in which all of the Lawrence paintings are hung. There have been reproductions of them in American and English art magazines the last few years, and a book was published just recently on Lawrence with reproductions of the paintings, so eventually some museum will take the whole collection for its historical interest.

Milton: In the hotel, isn't there a sign saying "For Adults Only" or some such thing?

Waters: Most of them are nudes, and some of the paintings were forcibly removed and banned in Europe. I don't pass any moral judgment on the subject matter—I think they are just not good paintings myself.

Milton: Well, Lawrence was all excited about symbolism—not abstract symbolism—

Waters: No—these are all figures of nudes.

Milton: Now, there is another painter. Is he from the earlier group—Berninghaus?

Waters: Charles Berninghaus was an early painter. He was a—as I recall—he came from St. Louis and like so many of the early painters, had commissions from magazines to come West and make live drawings for their illustrations, which was wonderful. Those old magazines with the beautiful illustrations instead of photographs—artists would come out commissioned by the Santa Fe Railroad or the Denver and Rio Grande. He liked Taos very much and established a studio and spent summers there for years before he finally moved there permanently. He was one of the old standbys.

Milton: Is he still there?

Waters: No, he died several years ago.

Milton: Is there some kind of noticeable feeling between the older painters who came there first, and the young ones who come in nowadays?

Waters: Oh yes, I think so. The old NA's—the National Academician, objective painters—are distinctively old-fashioned, and the new ones are trying to be modern in their painting. So it's the old clash between the old and the new.

Milton: Yes. Now you have said that two of the big ones came from Russia, one by way of Paris. Are there any—?

Waters: And one from England.

Milton: Yes.

Waters: Which shows the metropolitan flavor.

Milton: Have there been any native painters coming out of the Taos environment?

Waters: No. Not a painter. But a very fine friend of ours, an illiterate Spanish wood carver—his name was Patrocino Barella—made his living hauling wood from the mountains and doing odd jobs, but was a natural-born sculptor in wood, and his stuff is now being acquired by museums and collectors all over. He used to wrap up his carvings in a newspaper and go from house to house, selling them for whatever he could get. He had several children and whenever he and his wife would have a fuss, she would kick him out and he would go out to a little hut in back—

Milton: This is the man who burned to death recently?

Waters: —Yes—and drink a little. It was evidently during one of these sprees that he went to bed with a cigarette—the whole place caught fire and he was burned in it. But I think he should be classed as one of Taos' artists. A real creative artist.

Milton: You would probably turn up a number of these people from the folk art level—the weavers, the carvers, the jewelry makers, etc. How about literature, have you ever run across a local Pueblo Indian or Spanish-American who has done any writing? Say poetry?

Waters: I can't recall, offhand. Ethnologists, in making studies of the prayers and chants, have got some very nice poetry—this constitutes real poetry—but as far as just individual poetry, I have never run into any. Undoubtedly they have it.

63

Six *

Milton: Up until about twenty years ago Master's and Ph.D. theses in universities were almost entirely devoted to British writers. I remember when I was an undergraduate looking forward to this, I had to fight the battle of American literature vs. British, and now, within a few years, we have finally recognized what is going on in the western half of America and are making this subject matter acceptable in our universities for the very first time. Karen Kling has, at the University of South Dakota at least, pioneered in this area by doing a Master's thesis on you, Frank. You haven't read it yet or seen it?

Waters: I'm quite complimented. No. I haven't seen it.

Milton: I remember parts of the struggle that you went through, Karen, in doing this. We would like to ask Frank some of the questions that stumped both of us while we were going through the material.

Kling: Well, one of the things I would like to ask about is the duality motif, as it is obvious in the Indian ceremonies, particularly in the Deer Dance. In *Masked Gods* you explained the dualism which is represented there, and I was wondering if you would explain this further. In *The Man Who Killed the Deer,* Martiniano watches the dance. What does he learn from it?

*Waters and Milton have been joined by Karen Kling.

Waters: The problem of human duality is of course too tall an order to fill here. Let's just say there are bi-polar tensions in man, in all life—male and female, reason and instinct, the conscious and unconscious, matter and spirit, etc. Their conflict has given us in the past our greatest trouble, and their reconciliation in the future is our greatest hope. To solve the problem of these opposites was the concern of the ancient Chinese yin and yang doctrine, of Christianity, and of the ancient Mexicans. Now in a previous interview here I made some comments on the deity of the Toltecs and Aztecs. Quetzalcoatl, the feathered serpent, embodied the quetzal bird, symbol of heaven and spirit, and the serpent coatl, symbol of earth and matter. The myth and symbolism about him is too involved to go into now, but by reconciling the opposites Quetzalcoatl became his people's Redeemer, as was the Christ of our Christianity, and established a religion that lasted a good twelve centuries. So it's obvious that centuries ago the Indians on this continent were aware of the problem of human duality. Now the Deer Dance of Taos Pueblo, still being given, is a mystery play and deals with this same problem. As you say, I talked about it in *Masked Gods*—its symbology. The two Deer Mothers symbolizing the female imperative, the instinctual forces of the unconscious, the earth. And the Deer Dancers, the men trying to break free from the circle, symbolizing the masculine intellect, the forces of the will of man. So there's a bi-polar tension here—whoops and yells, scrambles in the snow, as one breaks free and is brought back by the Deer Watchers, etc. A lot of fun, a drama of what takes place inside us. All to show, as I see it, that we excessively rational white Anglo-Americans by our force of will really can't break free from the forces of the unconscious, from the realm of instinct embodied within us. We've got to reconcile the two. And this is what I tried to show that Martiniano felt in *The Man Who Killed the Deer*—that he'd gone too far and had to come back to his own roots.

Kling: In *The Yogi of Cockroach Court,* the girl's name was Guadalupe. Now was she purposely named this? Wasn't this the name also of the Earth mother of the Aztecs?

Waters: Sure, that's what she originally was. Tonantzin, Aztec goddess of the earth and corn. When the early Spanish people came and found that all the Indian people in Mexico were worshipping her, they simply changed her name to Guadalupe and made her a proper saint. So she still remains the patroness of all Indian Mexico.

Milton: Where does Guadalupe really get to at the end of that novel? A number of people have asked about her.

Waters: She reaches a dead end.

Milton: Do you think this is symbolic, or is this an individual matter?

Waters: No, it is individual, not symbolic.

Milton: This is one difficulty in attempting to read because there may be a lot of symbolism.

Waters: Not here—just a coincidence of names. It's difficult to write any novel and carry out complete symbolism because then it is no longer a novel. You can carry it for a while, but the character sooner or later takes over as a living person. And that's what happened in this case.

Kling: Another character—Barby. Was the half-breed in him symbolized by his defiance and so on?

Waters: Typified, not symbolized. I was primarily interested in doing that book after having done one on Indians and one on the Spanish colonial people still remaining in New Mexico. I wanted to write one on the mixed blood types, and these two characters I chose from the Mexican border area, which is full of such racial mixtures.

Kling: Were they patterned after any particular characters? Was there anyone like Guadalupe, for example?

Waters: Well, I know a couple of girls down there—they were both percentage girls. I don't know what you would call them now, but—

Milton: Call girls—in the hotels.

Waters: No, there were too many cribs full of prostitutes. They would hang out in a huge casino where there were gambling and dining and dancing, and they would float around and dance and they would be paid so much for every dance by the customer. Their main job was to get their partners to buy drinks. From all this they'd get a percentage, which is how they made their living. Some of these casinos and cantinas in those days were very lush affairs. The wines were all imported from Spain and Portugal, paying no duty in Mexico. They had wonderful food, always venison, quail, dove, wild turkey—and wonderful and quite good entertainment. They had entertainers from Mexico. During the big boom in Imperial Valley on both sides of the border, Mexicali was quite a place, and this character Guadalupe was modeled on a couple of the girls I had become acquainted with.

Kling: Another thing I was curious about. In one of the later chapters in *Masked Gods,* you correlate atomic energy research experiments in Los Alamos, New Mexico with Pueblo Indian ceremonialism—the idea of the Rain Dance converting energy into matter, and the atomic experiments converting matter into energy. And with a non-scientific mind, I really didn't quite understand it.

Waters: Oh, I think that probably is a literary parallel, but there are too many parallels there in that section of the country to ignore. I don't suppose there's such a close juxtaposition of the technological future with the prehistoric past anywhere else in the world. There's the tremendous complex of the Los Alamos Scientific Laboratory which covers seventy-seven square miles—laboratories strung out all over. In that same area you have dozens of prehistoric pueblos, most of which have not been excavated. So you have the new and the old juxtaposed so closely. One thing always amused me—at Los Alamos they always tried to hire neighboring peoples if they could. As no one could live in Los Alamos unless he were working on the secret project, secretaries and any kind of clerical help was at a premium, so all the scientists' wives pitched in to get a job. Now to take care of the house and the children, the government would send trucks down the hill and would bring up truck loads of Spanish and Indian maids. They also tried to give as much work as possible to the Indians of the San Ildefonso and Santa Clara pueblos, but occasionally all the men would not show up because it was the day of a ceremonial dance so they had to do their duties and stay home.

Milton: Now, at the atomic laboratories, aren't they trying in a sense to get at the core of physical life? Aren't they proceeding mentally to a one-piece—?

Waters: I think so. That's the aim of science now. It's reducing matter to smaller and smaller units or whatever you call them. A molecule to an atom and an atom broken into electrons and protons and on down. And they will probably reach the point where matter doesn't exist. Simply a stress and strain in energy.

Milton: Is this consistent with the Indian thinking going on right outside the atomic laboratories?

Waters: I think there is a very close parallel because of the Indian belief that there is no such thing as inanimate matter, that all matter is imbued with life and energy, although it's in a very low form. Animals haven't evolved to the same point as mankind, nor does plant life reach the state of animals, yet everything, the earth and mountains, is imbued with energy, with life in some degree.

Milton: The reason I ask is that their ceremonialism becomes elaborate, seems to diversify rather than to push in to the core. But is this simply a different way of getting at the same thing?

Waters: It's probably the same thing, because if you have a vast universe outside, you have a vast universe within the atom. One the small and one the large.

Milton: And if you embrace it all through ceremonial mysticism you will accomplish the same thing. We were going to bring up the same question, I think, in connection with the mountains in Colorado again.

Kling: Well, yes. In *The Colorado* you write about the effect of the land, the spirit of place, I believe you call it, the effect the mountains had on the mountain men who were the first Europeans to live here for a period of time. They became more "savage," for example, than the Indians. Do you think this was entirely the influence of the land?

Waters: I think these mountain men were a strange breed. They all seem very strange to us because there was no rational reason for a man from the East to break away from his family, his children, his home town, and to immure himself alone in the mountains with a pinch of salt, a few traps, and a bearskin to cover him, and live alone for months or years. What was he after? I don't know. What they were hunting for, I don't know, but it was not for the few bales of beaver that they trapped.

Kling: They wouldn't save their money anyway, would they?

Waters: No, they would make a great deal of money, selling all their bales of beaver, go on one big spree and then back to the mountains, alone. This was their reaction to this ambivalent spirit of place of a new continent.

Milton: Do you remember one incident about Kit Carson when he was in the northern Rockies with, I think, about sixty men, and they were attacked by a group of Indians, and he left more men to guard their furs than he took out with him to meet the Indians?

This suggests a gross materialism at the expense of human life. How do you correlate that with the other?

Waters: Some of these big companies that employed men as company trappers were a great deal different from a lone free trapper. Up in the north especially, these large trading companies controlled the fur trade, but south around Taos were mostly the free, solitary trappers.

Kling: Taos was once a center wasn't it?

Waters: Yes, there were two main trapping and trading centers. One was the famous Green River Rendezvous on the border of Colorado and Wyoming, and the other one was Taos. Of course, Santa Fe and Taos got very well known because the Santa Fe Trail offered an outlet carrying their furs back to the Missouri River for sale.

Kling: Did the mountain men ever believe like the Indians in the spirit of place imbuing the mountains and the animals and plants?

Waters: Well, according to record, most of them adopted Indian beliefs, blew smoke to the four directions, and acted very much like Indians.

Kling: I wonder if they actually believed it or if it was—

Waters: Yes. There were such fabulous characters among mountain men. There has been so much written about them, but the peculiar urge, what it was they were after, what they were—this has never quite been gone into.

Milton: You suggested that you didn't particularly care, right now, to go into this in another novel. Any reason for that?

Waters: No. That just doesn't appeal to me right now.

Kling: Do you know what your next novel would be about at all?

Waters: No. I have been very much interested the last few years in the state of Chihuahua and Sonora, those two states along the Sierra Madre in northern Mexico. That's the last great wilderness, I think, on this continent.

Kling: You told us a little bit about it in the last book of the trilogy, which was very interesting.

Waters: I would like to do a novel on that region. I have been down there many, many times the past few years.

Milton: Do you have any feeling that the impression that D.H. Lawrence left us of Mexico needs to be corrected?

Kling: That's just what I was going to ask.

Waters: I think conditions are different.

Milton: This would be a contemporary theme that you would use?

Waters: Probably. Although I think Lawrence's sketches in *Mornings in Mexico* are very lovely, and his novel, *The Plumed Serpent* has great descriptive power. But I would like to do something on that area which is not written about. Really not very much is known of this vast wilderness of Chihuahua and Sonora, which is divided by the crest of the Sierra Madres. Until two years ago there were no roads through there, hardly any way to get through except by pack animals. Now there is a new little narrow-gauge railroad that goes from Chihuahua to the Pacific Coast port of Topolobompo, clear over the crest of the Sierras and down through the jungle. It skirts the wonderful canyon called the Barranea de Cobre, which is a quarter mile deeper and probably much longer than the 283-mile-long Grand Canyon. Undoubtedly, within the next few years, it will be one of the greatest scenic trips on this continent, but still it is all wild country.

Milton: Would the type of character that you pick down there be similar—at least somewhat similar—to those in *People of the Valley?*

Waters: Yes. I think they would be very similar to those on our frontier here soon after the Civil War—but Mexican-Indians.

Milton: Is this anywhere in the region of the little Mormon community that you mentioned was isolated?

Waters: Yes. Around Casas Grandes. There will be a road through there, I think, within a few years. A very delightful spot. Soon after the Civil War some Mormons from Salt Lake got permission from Mexico to settle in the little valley out from Casas Grandes, so for almost a century they have been there and have developed their own brick kilns, built little Mormon houses of red brick, and are a very tidy people. They have lived there all this time, and speak English as well as Spanish, and it's a strange little community to run into.

Milton: They are isolated, in a sense, within a Spanish community. And you have stressed the fact in the *Book of the Hopi* that the Hopi Indians are isolated within the Navaho Reservation which is isolated within the Anglo community. Now, back again to the mountain men who lived in isolation. Does this perhaps turn out to be the big theme of the West for literature?

Waters: Well, it certainly gets back to the theme of all our talks here. Because mountain people are different from plains and prairie people, due to their enclosure, of being immured in solitude. Even along the upper Rio Grande in New Mexico we refer to the Rio Arriba as different from the lower river, for in the lower reaches of the river and the plains and fertile bottom lands the people are more peaceful. But up there you find all the strange religious cults. In the mountains. This is where your strange cults thrive. Like the Penitentes and the Indian pueblos and the Anglo individualists, painters and crackpots.

73

Kling: I was wondering, is it ever possible for the white man to really understand the Indian? Byers—I think of *The Man Who Killed the Deer*—had lived with Indians and was close to them all his life, and yet, at times, he feels left out, and he is left out in times of crisis in the tribe. Is it possible to really understand the feelings that they have in their religion?

Waters: Oh, probably not wholly. I know a very fine ethnologist who has done some beautiful books on Plains Indian tribes, who went to the Hopi country and lived there for two years to do a study on the Hopi, but left because she could never feel at home among them.

Kling: Don't they sometimes laugh at the white man?

Waters: Oh, sure.

Kling: I think of the dances—you told in one of your books how they make fun of our time-consciousness and so on.

Waters: And occasionally I think you run into resentment against the whites.

Milton: Do you feel that you have to maintain your own isolation up in Arroyo Seco in order to keep in tune with Western attitudes that you have lived up to?

Waters: Oh, I think it's a matter—just a matter of working. A man who makes his living sitting at a typewriter has certainly got to be alone to work. I think he could go it just as well in a New York bedroom. New York to me is a very lonely place. You can be more lonely in New York and more let alone, than any place I know of. But the isolation in nature of a more or less primitive people, people I have been interested in, is a different thing. This question of immuration or isolation in mountain areas is a peculiar thing.

Milton: Would you make a distinction between loneliness and aloneness?

Waters: Yes. Aloneness, I think, doesn't mean loneliness.

Milton: For the people who are living in this area?

Waters: Yes. As a matter of fact, I think the whole Mormon empire was a large example. The whole empire, the whole people, a religion, an autocracy that was set down in the midst of a great wilderness and that bore no relationship to anything in America.

Kling: I think you talked about their violence in one of the books and the reason for this—something I had never realized before— that it was the effect of the land and their aloneness between groups.

Waters: That's because—a white group—whereas the Penitente cult is a Spanish group—but both had that same violence and guilt and the need for atonement.

Kling: The way a half-breed feels, alone. Aloneness. He doesn't go on.

Milton: What would he be atoning for personally?

Waters: The half-breed? Oh, I don't know. I sometimes wonder if a half-breed isn't straddling the fence. He is pulled from both directions.

Milton: I wonder if that isn't all there is to it, for him at least. Although we could make subject matter out of it in a different way. You know, almost everybody in America is a mixed-breed, which is something we forget about.

Waters: Of many different kinds. What a true American is I wouldn't know. All of us have so many strains.

Milton: But in the city literature we get, oh, sometimes racial inter-marriages—not too often, it's usually economic statuses we bring together—so perhaps the true kind of half-breed is better indicated in the Spanish-American contact in the Southwest than in any-thing in the northern part of the country.

Seven *

Milton: The area that Frederick Manfred (who is with us here) is writing about is largely flat—it's the plains country, very few mountains.

Manfred: Except for *Riders of Judgment* which has the Big Horns in it. It's flat enough though. I write mostly about the flat. I wrote mostly about where the cowboys—

Milton: It's the cow country. You use a rather tall hill at least to bring Cain into the story. Is there some special symbolism in that?

Manfred: Yes, I'd say so. I really hadn't thought about it, but of course a writer often wonders how he should enter a story to catch the reader's attention. I wanted a way different from what goes on in most cowboy stories. Maybe I did have a symbol in mind here. Man comes out of obscurity and goes back into obscurity. Or, it's like the spirit that comes down from above and goes to earth for a while, into flesh, and then comes back out.

Milton: This is a curious distinction between the kind of nebulousness of the clouds that you were concerned with there and Frank's Rogier going deep into the heart of Pike's Peak. That's as solid as the—as solid on the one hand as the clouds are flimsy on the other—and I am wondering—

*Waters and Milton have been joined by novelist Frederick Manfred.

Manfred: There's a definite distinction between the two. One is preoccupation with space and the other with depth. They are both inquiries. Going from what we are to something else.

Milton: If the space comes from the plains, as it does by definition, then the person who is attracted to the mountains or particularly interested in them is concerned always with a matter of depth. Or, more obviously, the height.

Waters: It seems to me that's a fundamental preoccupation, depth or height. The spire of the Christian church and the subterranean Indian kiva.

Manfred: Yes.

Waters: All these miners that always want to go into the deepest canyon.

Manfred: In other words, you start from a high place. Of course, I start from a high place in this particular book. I never thought of that.

Milton: You suggested that a plains character or plains writer often can be frustrated. If he is concerned with heights and depths and he is out on this big flat, what is this going to do to him?

Manfred: Well, he is going to build towers on these plains, or look within his soul and go down.

Milton: In other words, individual introspection quite apart from the landscape.

Manfred: The place where I live, over in Luverne, was an old mountain, maybe a mile and a half high. The top was shaved off a long time ago. Sometimes in my more grandiose, perhaps foolish, moments I think that I went back and put my home on this old mountain site because I was going to put the mountain back, in the form of books.

Milton: That's figurative.

Manfred: Figurative, yes. We do not necessarily have the range put back there.

Waters: But do we have any plains malady that corresponds to what we know as mountain cabin fever? Two men in a cabin— that's where the name comes from you know—closed in by cabin fever. Well, of course, whole groups, tribes, have cabin fever in the mountains because they may be enclosed in a mountain range or they may be a whole race of people that are immured in the mountains, inbred for many years.

Milton: Well, this same term is used in the Minnesota woods, but I have not heard it applied to the sod hut in Nebraska.

Manfred: In those sodbuster huts on the open plains the men didn't get cabin fever. But the women did, in a reverse way. Beret in *Giants in the Earth* got space fever. Too much space.

Waters: Well, see, there is a difference between—you see, one draws out and the other drives in. I don't know of any group of people on the wide open plains that have all of the strange psychological compulsions of the early Mormons in Utah or these strange communities like the Penitentes in the canyons. These are two ethnic groups, large groups, both compressed by the mountains.

Milton: Now, at the same time, isn't there in the mountains some kind of mysticism which accompanies the upthrust feeling? It certainly appeared in Clarence King and John Muir, the early naturalists who went out and described the Sierra Nevadas.

Waters: I think mysticism is a perception peculiar to the mountain-bred.

Milton: Why so, other than this simple notion of height?

Waters: I don't know unless it's this immuration. If you want to get a chemical reaction, you close something in a retort and heat it. Well, when you take a small group of people, close them in a mountain canyon that's blocked through the winter, they are in a retort, and something happens. Whereas, if you are out on the plains, that pressure is driving psychological forces outward.

Milton: Except on the plains you have the dust storms that some-times enclose you, make you feel alone—and snowstorms.

Manfred: When snow covers your house, though, you are only six or seven feet down. You know that when the storm is over you can dig out. You are free again. And you can roam. I just wonder how far back these feelings go into our heritage. There's a theory in anthropology about two kinds of shelters in ancient days. One is the natural shelter of caves, in mountains, and the other is a shelter that is built on the open land. The cave man eventually became a city dweller in a house or maybe still finds his home in the moun-tains. The one with the heritage of the plains still prefers the plains.

Waters: That's the difference, probably, between the nomad and the village dweller.

Milton: In literature does this mean that we are going to be stuck for a long, long time with the plains literature of the kind of *O Pioneers, Giants in the Earth,* and what have you—these depress-ing stories—in contrast to the possibilities that exist in the moun-tains? If we try to encompass this whole thing as Western—

Manfred: May I comment on that?

Milton: Yes.

Manfred: We got these depressing stories from people who origi-nally came from the cities. Rölvaag was a Norwegian who came from the tight fjords of the small cities in Norway. Hamlin Gar-land was not reared in South Dakota where he wrote those terribly depressing things, but in the East where there was a sense of community. He didn't really understand; or he wasn't really a voice of authority. And Willa Cather was raised in Virginia, and the contrast of the place of her formative years with what she found in Nebraska led to those novels that were unhappy. But I don't see why anyone should be unhappy on the plains. I like open spaces, and I like roving in the summertime. On a true prairie you can find a new flower each day and your life seems to go on forever. I don't think we are going to be stuck forever with sad novels from the plains.

Milton: Well, I wonder then if *all* these depressing novels were written by Easterners? As a generalization?

Manfred: By invaders. The Sioux Indian could have written them. True nomad.

Milton: Would they all be optimistic then?

Manfred: Oh, they wouldn't be concerned one way or the other. It just would be a marvelous evocation of their life. And we reading them would think this is it. A moving experience.

Milton: Yes, because this would result in a kind of exuberance.

Manfred: A natural exuberance.

Milton: If this natural exuberance should exist throughout the West, why, for example, would some of the Southwestern Indians take peyote? Would this have anything to do with removing a natural impression?

Waters: I think the peyote religion is an escape religion because it did not come into the Southwest until the pressure was put on these Indian groups by us white people. So it offered an escape. It was the same thing as the Ghost Dance among the Sioux many years ago; it offered an escape mechanism.

Milton: But this is not an escape from their natural environment. It's an escape from the new—?

Waters: It's a psychological escape. Peyote predominantly instigates very beautiful dreams. Actually, peyote is an escape mechanism and as long as people have their own valid religion, a peyote man doesn't have much of a chance. Now they have tried it in some of the pueblos and for fiteeen or twenty years they were strong, but it hasn't lasted. It hasn't outlasted the native old religion, but it has spread quite a bit to other tribes, like the Navahos, in the very measure under which they live.

Milton: This doesn't just intensify their own religion then, it's something completely different. Would you be against it because it is an escape mechanism?

Waters: Yes, I think so. I think that religion can't be founded on an artificial source. I think a religion has to grow right out of the earth and be absorbed completely with the whole mythical content of the unconscious. But to take a—I can't call it a narcotic because it hasn't been proved to have narcotic qualities, but it certainly induces—induces dreams and color vision.

Milton: But the drug itself comes out of the earth. Couldn't you say that this is a means—?

Waters: Sort of like opium. Alcohol.

Milton: Yes. How do you get past natural elements?

Waters: I don't know of any religion that is founded on alcohol or marijuana or on opium.

Manfred: In the old days they had mead during the spring ritual when rules and taboos were broken. That really isn't religion; that's more a celebration.

Waters: That's an escape mechanism that isn't used perpetually as a way of life.

Manfred: That's right. I had an experience about the peyote things. I didn't mind that they used it, myself, because the Christian people have alcohol in the Lord's Supper. I don't think they took enough alcohol in the Lord's Supper to change the tone or complexion of the taking of the Holy Sacrament, but nevertheless they had alcohol in it. So I thought, well, let the Indian have his little natural drug. They call it the American Church, don't they?

Waters: The Native American Church, but that was a tag hung on it by the government.

Manfred: Oh, I see.

Waters: The government sponsored this, which was a very peculiar thing to me, that the United States Government, the Indian Bureau, would officially sponsor this, the American Indian Church, and give it that name—The Native American Indian Church.

Manfred: But I thought that out of this eventually they might drop off this part of it, and the mere fact of having congregated through this medium that eventually they would have a native Indian church of some kind. This is what they hoped, isn't it?

Waters: I'll tell you, it has a peculiar history. I don't want to talk too much about it because I am from New Mexico where many of the people take peyote and many of my friends are peyote eaters. Peyote originated among the Huichole Indians in the Sierra Madre mountains in Mexico and then it spread up into the plains tribes. The Kiowas brought the peyote button to Taos Pueblo and there was a great Peyote movement twenty-five years ago. It still has members, but it is dying out. It is not like it was fifteen years ago. But, on the other hand, it has moved westward and has been adopted by the Navahos, and now I understand it is moving north to the Sioux. Following the course of this, it has followed the deterioration of Indian culture as a substitute for their own valid religion which has broken down.

Manfred: Maybe that's why the government sponsored it, as a diversion to break up the old religion.

Waters: But that follows right on the heels of the native ceremonialism.

Manfred: And this we really should preserve—the old ceremonialism.

Waters: That's the reason why I have not believed in it.

83

Milton: Hasn't that ceremonialism lasted longer in the Southwest than it has farther north? Why would the peyote cult start down there? You said as a substitute for the old ceremonialism.

Waters: The Huicholes are dying out, and then it spread to the Kiowas on the Great Plains, and now the Kiowas are dying out.

Manfred: Oh, yes, and they are almost gone.

Waters: It came to the Pueblos where ceremonialism was very strong, so it didn't last very long. Then it spread through the Navahos as their ceremonialism began to break up. For a different reason, not because they are so poor, but because they are getting too rich—uranium royalties, oil royalties, timber and coal. They are getting to be the richest Indian tribe in the country.

Manfred: And this stuff is almost autonomous. I mean there is more and more of it becoming autonomous down there now. You can see it when you look at them. They are well dressed, they are a rich tribe, probably one of the richest minority groups in the United States.

Milton: Well, Fred, have you found anything like this when you have been talking with the Sioux while doing research for *Conquering Horse* and *Lord Grizzly* and so on?

Manfred: Well, the Yanktons are pretty well gone—the Yankton Sioux. There are some Yanktonai left, the tribe that Oscar Howe comes from, up on the Missouri. But the Yanktons are gone around Greenwood. The peyote button didn't come up here soon enough for them to pick it up.

Waters: You can find a great deal of argument against those that I have given and a very fine spokesman is the late Aldous Huxley. Because Aldous Huxley experimented and took peyote. He has written two or three books about it and is a very staunch believer in it, but Huxley was always experimenting as an extreme rationalist with extrasensory perception, for he was very much interested in this release.

Manfred: His arguments wouldn't be Indian. His arguments would be of a white man who has come to this extremity and wants some new excitement.

Waters: And the drug distilled from it is now being used as a medicine.

Milton: This all sounds like a revival of the kind of thing Mary Austin, Lawrence, and Jeffers, to a certain extent, dealt with back in the twenties and thirties when they were trying to almost legislate man out of the environment and get back to a concentration on the land itself.

Waters: Now, there is a great deal of interest in these hallucinogenic mushrooms. They have been found only in a few parts of Mexico. The use of peyote intensifies the color, but I understand that the hallucinogenic mushrooms induce dreams that break down our horizontal—our conception of time as a horizontal stream. They have to do with bridging all time periods.

Manfred: It seems to me, though, in some things I read about primitive religions that alcoholic beverages were very closely associated with religious rites.

Waters: Well, they were in Mexico because you find in old Aztec codices written before the Spaniards first came, early in the 1500s, accounts of both hallucinogenic mushrooms and peyote.

Manfred: And the Druids in England, before the Anglo-Saxons moved in, used an alcoholic liquor of some kind to get them to the proper frenzy for their religious rites. It isn't actually too strange to use alcoholic beverages or some outside influence to have your religious frenzy.

Waters: No, because the essence of all primitive religions lies in breaking through the transcendent boundary, and all these helpful aids were used to enable them to break into a greater community.

Manfred: And to get into this sense of a community they are all alike for a little while—the greater community—they were all alike for a little while.

Milton: Is anyone trying to do this sort of thing in literature? That you know of? If this happens to be a Western characteristic of some kind, breaking things down into images, into the subconscious, what do we do with the strong story line?

Waters: Well, the Western story line adheres to the past almost rigidly. So far there is a stock Western thing, you know.

Manfred: Sophocles and Euripides had a stock Greek—old Greek—line.

Waters: Well, I have always maintained that here in America we have an indigenous art form equivalent to it—equivalent to the Greek drama—that's the Cowboy-Indian thriller. The great American Morality Play. That's quite firmly inbred into our motion pictures, our novels—the Cowboy vs. the Indian. The triumph of good over evil.

Manfred: And the Greek uses the Dionysius goat theme which came out of the celebration of certain rites every spring, of the solstice, etc. And then they elaborated this into plays later on. The simple thing which became a complex thing. Well, maybe we are just at the beginning of something that's worthwhile.

Milton: Well, Frank is one of the few Western writers who hasn't dealt with the Cowboy-Indian story.

Waters: No. I believe this is so old-fashioned.

Milton: Everyone else has tried it to a certain extent.

Manfred: Well, Frank, you are probably in the right mood to write the good one. If you have that attitude, you might be—

Waters: I would love to get into the mood if I knew how.

Manfred: You might be exactly the one.

Waters Bibliography

NOVELS

The Wild Earth's Nobility, New York: Liveright Publishing Corp.,
1935.
Below Grass Roots, New York: Liveright Publishing Corp., 1937.
Dust Within the Rock, New York: Farrar and Rinehart, 1940.
People of the Valley, New York: Farrar and Rinehart, 1941.
—, Denver: Alan Swallow, Publisher, 1962.
—, Chicago: The Swallow Press, 1969.
The Man Who Killed the Deer, New York: Farrar and Rinehart,
1942.
—, Denver: University of Denver Press, 1951.
—, Denver, Alan Swallow, Publisher, 1954.
—, Hamburg: Christian Wegner Verlag, 1959. Translated as *Mar-
tiniano und der Hirsch.*
—, London: Neville Spearman Ltd., 1962.
—, Paris: Albin Michelle Editions, 1964. Translated as *L'Homme
Qui a Tué le Cerf.*
—, Flagstaff: Northland Press, 1965. Illustrated, limited, signed
edition.
—, Chicago: The Swallow Press, 1968, 1970.
—, New York: Pocket Books, 1971.
The Yogi of Cockroach Court, New York: Rinehart & Co., 1947.
—, Chicago: The Swallow Press. Forthcoming.
The Woman at Otowi Crossing, Denver: Alan Swallow, Publisher,
1966.
—, Chicago: The Swallow Press, 1971.
Pike's Peak: A Family Saga, Chicago: The Swallow Press, 1971.
(Completely re-written, one-volume novel based on *The Wild
Earth's Nobility, Below Grass Roots*, and *Dust Within the
Rock*.)

NON-FICTION

The Colorado, Rivers of America Series, New York: Farrar and Rinehart, 1946.
—, New York: Rinehart and Company, 1959.
Masked Gods: Navaho and Pueblo Ceremonialism, Albuquerque: University of New Mexico Press, 1950.
—, Denver: Alan Swallow, Publisher, 1962.
—, Chicago: The Swallow Press, 1970.
—, New York: Ballantine Books, 1970.
Book of the Hopi, New York: The Viking Press, 1963.
—, New York: Ballantine Books, 1969.
Pumpkin Seed Point, Chicago: The Swallow Press, 1969.

BIOGRAPHY

Midas of the Rockies, New York: Covici-Friede, 1937. Biography of Winfield Scott Stratton, discoverer of Cripple Creek.
—, Denver: University of Denver Press, 1949.
—, Denver: Alan Swallow, Publisher, 1954.
—, Chicago: The Swallow Press, 1972.
The Earp Brothers of Tombstone, New York: Clarkson N. Potter, 1960.
—, London: Neville Spearman, Ltd., 1962.
—, London: Transworld Publications, 1963.

ART MONOGRAPH

Leon Gaspard, Flagstaff: Northland Press, 1964.

SHORT FICTION AND NON-FICTION

"Easy Meat." *North American Review*, April 1931. Story.
"Navajo Yei-Bet-Chai." *Yale Review*, Spring 1939.
"The Magic that Persists." *The Southwest Review*, Summer 1947.

"Crucible of Conflict." *The New Mexico Quarterly Review*, Autumn 1948.

"Navajo Trading Posts." *The New Mexico Quarterly Review*, Winter 1948.

"The Navajo Missions." *New Mexico Quarterly*, Spring 1950.

"Indian Influence on Taos Art." *New Mexico Quarterly*, Summer 1951.

"Nicolai Fechin." *Arizona Highways*, February 1952.

"The Roaring Colorado." *Holiday Magazine*, August 1954.

"The Mystery of Mesa Verde." *Holiday Magazine*, September 1955.

"Tucson." *Holiday Magazine*, October 1956.

"The Canyon." *Arizona Highways*, June 1960.

"The Colorado Is an Outlaw." *Arizona Highways*, June 1958. Reprinted from *The Colorado*.

The Sketches of Leon Gaspard. Los Angeles: Southwest Museum, 1962. Booklet.

"Two Views of Nature: White and Indian." *The South Dakota Review*, May 1964.

"The Western Novel: A Symposium." *The South Dakota Review*, Autumn 1964.

Introduction to *The Arapahoe Way* by Arthur Bass. New York: Clarkson N. Potter, 1966.

Mysticism and Witchcraft. Fine Arts Series, Fort Collins: Colorado State University, 1966. Booklet.

"Notes on Alan Swallow." *Denver Quarterly*, Spring 1967.

"Quetzalcoatl Versus D.H. Lawrence's *Plumed Serpent.*" *Western American Literature*, Summer 1968.

"Words." *Western American Literature*, Fall 1968.

"Michio Takayama." Catalogue for Exhibition, Palm Springs Desert Museum, 1969.

Introduction to *Oo-oonah Art*. Taos Pueblo Indian School, 1970.

"Zuni Pueblo." *New Mexico Magazine*, November-December 1971.

"The Man Who Killed the Deer—Thirty Years Later." *New Mexico Magazine*, January-February 1972.

BOOK REVIEWS

Regular contributor of reviews of major books on the West. *Saturday Review*, 1950-1956.

EDITORIALS

Two editorials weekly for *El Crepusculo*. Taos, New Mexico, 1950-1951.

TELEVISION

Seven 30-minute conversations with John R. Milton taped in the studios of KUSD-TV, University of South Dakota, November 1964. These tapes are part of a library of video tapes of conversations with the major Western American novelists of the mid-twentieth century.

SELECTED ARTICLES ABOUT WATERS

Bucco, Martin. *Frank Waters*. Southwest Writers Series, no. 22. Austin: Steck-Vaughn Company, 1969.

Lyon, Thomas J. "An Ignored Meaning of the West." *Western American Literature*, Spring 1968.

Milton, John R. "The Western Novel: Sources and Forms." *Chicago Review*, Summer 1963.

—, "The American West: A Challenge to the Literary Imagination." *Western American Literature*, Winter 1967.

—, "The Land as Form in Frank Waters and William Eastlake." *Kansas Quarterly*, Spring 1970.

Pilkington, William T. "Character and Landscape: Frank Waters' Colorado Trilogy." *Western American Literature*, Fall 1967.

Swallow, Alan. "The Mavericks." *Critique*, Winter 1959.

Young, Vernon. "Frank Waters: Problems of the Regional Imperative." *New Mexico Quarterly Review*, Autumn 1949.

Milton, John R
    Conversations with Frank Waters, edited by John R
Milton. ₁1st ed.₁ Chicago, Sage Books ₁c1971₁

90 p. Illus. 23 cm. $4.00

14 11/08

Bibliography : p. 87–90.